More Praise for *Big Social Mobile*

"Put simply, your business likely doesn't understand your customers nearly well enough. *Big Social Mobile* provides startling insights and a simple blueprint for smart brands looking to build strong, loyal relationships with their customers."

—Larry Drebes, CEO and CTO, Janrain

"As a mobile first company, we're always educating our customers about why a multifaceted mobile strategy is key to their continued evolution. *Big Social Mobile* is a great springboard to a mobile first approach and will help readers guide their companies into the future."

—Irfan Mohammed, Co-founder, Personagraph

"Organizations today are still in the early stages of determining how to apply social media, big data, mobile technology, and other digital initiatives in a way that fits with their existing business model. *Big Social Mobile* is a must read on how to use these evolving technologies and methods to achieve a competitive edge while avoiding the pitfalls they often present."

—Gary Cokins, Founder, Analytics-Based Performance
Management LLC and co-author of
Business Predictive Analytics

"David has bridged the gap between the disparate worlds of big data and enterprise information to establish new fundamentals that executives and specialized practitioners alike should learn. Applying these will help ensure that enterprises remain competitive and can easily adapt to the rapidly changing environments around them."

—Claudia Imhoff, Founder, Boulder Business
Intelligence Brain Trust

BIG
SOCIAL
MOBILE

Previous works by David F. Giannetto

The Performance Power Grid: The Proven Method to Create and Sustain Superior Organizational Performance

The Decoy Artist: America's Last Hunter-Carver (New Jersey Council for the Humanities Book of the Year Nominee)

BIG
SOCIAL
MOBILE

How Digital Initiatives Can Reshape the Enterprise and Drive Business Results

DAVID F. GIANNETTO

palgrave
macmillan

First published in 2014 by
PALGRAVE MACMILLAN®
in the United States—a division of St. Martin's Press LLC,
175 Fifth Avenue, New York, NY 10010.

Where this book is distributed in the UK, Europe and the rest of the world,
this is by Palgrave Macmillan, a division of Macmillan Publishers Limited,
registered in England, company number 785998, of Houndmills,
Basingstoke, Hampshire RG21 6XS.

Palgrave Macmillan is the global academic imprint of the above companies
and has companies and representatives throughout the world.

Palgrave® and Macmillan® are registered trademarks in the United States,
the United Kingdom, Europe and other countries.

ISBN: 978–1–137–41039–9

Library of Congress Cataloging-in-Publication Data

Giannetto, David F., 1968–
    Big social mobile : how digital initiatives can reshape the enterprise
and drive business results / David F. Giannetto.
      pages cm
    Includes bibliographical references and index.
    ISBN 978–1–137–41039–9 (hardback) —
    ISBN 1–137–41039–6 (hardback)
      1. Electronic commerce. 2. Social media. 3. Mobile communication
systems. 4. Big data. 5. Customer services. I. Title.

HF5548.32.G52 2014
658'.05—dc23   2014023063

A catalogue record of the book is available from the British Library.

Design by Newgen Knowledge Works (P) Ltd., Chennai, India.

First edition: December 2014

10 9 8 7 6 5 4 3 2 1

Printed in the United States of America.

For my parents.

CONTENTS

FIGURES

ACKNOWLEDGMENTS

ANYONE WHO HAS WORKED WITH SOCIAL media, mobile technology, or big data knows that any of these subjects alone could fill volumes. Taking on a project that combined them would have been impossible without the support of so many different people, organizations, and clients over the past several years. Foremost, Laurie Harting and her great staff at Palgrave Macmillan, and Bruce Wexler, an agent that has stuck by me through multiple books of wildly various subjects and genres. All of the professionals at Salient Management Company who have pursued a shared dream of changing how companies manage for over 30 years—I'm proud that I have been able to pursue it with you. Those who started as mentors, clients, or professors and became friends: Dale Carpenter, Jim Merrill, Ron Watkins, Mark Dombroski, Rodney Lovlie, Scott McNulty, Art Prompibalcheep, Sharan Jagpal, Gary Cokins, Eric Amadeo, Ayall Schanzer, and Byron Mignanelli. And most especially to Amy Howard for her support during all of the hours I spent away writing—the passion with which you pursue your dream is inspiring. Also my family, especially my sister Amy for her courage, and my parents, to whom this book is dedicated.

INTRODUCTION

AS I WRITE THIS, I'M FLYING FROM NEWARK, New Jersey, to Las Vegas on a major airline, sitting in the first-class section. Trish, a flight attendant, approaches me after takeoff, smiles, and says, "Hello, Mr. Giannetto, will you be joining us for lunch?" She turns to the two women with Russian accents across the aisle and asks them both the same question, also addressing them by name. Perhaps because I spend a great deal of my life working with companies to help make them customer-centric, information-driven, highly integrated enterprises, I notice that Trish is doing everything she can to make sure she personally connects with each passenger. She addresses all of us by name and seems genuinely interested in every passenger to whom she speaks.

When I ask Trish about her personalized approach, she explains that it's a result of her training and she takes it to heart. No doubt, her employer recognizes the value of customers in first class having a positive experience. Frequent flyers take the service they receive seriously, but they usually don't call the airline's customer service department when they have a complaint.

They don't have to—not anymore.

The most senior of travelers—the Global Alliance or 1k travelers—will receive a text from the airline asking about in-flight service before they even make it up the airplane's exit ramp. And they'll respond. If Trish doesn't address them by name, they may well report this omission, and a complaint will be logged in her file and she'll be counseled next time she checks in for a flight.

Training attendants to personalize service and retraining them when they don't are not new processes. What's new, though, is the use of technology to make the process happen in real time to improve the customer experience. This airline recognized that when these customers didn't have a good experience they—their most influential customers—were tarnishing their brand online, via social media and mobile technology, to their most profitable market segment.

The airline's social media analysts were the first to spot and respond to this dissatisfaction among their best customers. They deleted negative comments on social feeds, directly messaged these dissatisfied customers to apologize on behalf of the company, and suggested they contact customer service to complain. But these actions didn't help. In fact, they often made matters worse because these customers would then post complaints about the poor customer service response and how useless the airline's apologies were.

This airline's initial response to the growing power of customers is typical. It demonstrates how digital initiatives—social media, mobile technology, and the resulting big data—are adopted. They are islands within their enterprise, segregated from the people, processes, technology, and information that make up what can now be considered traditional enterprise functions: Sales, Operations, and other core departments. Increasingly, though, employees who work within these segregated digital initiatives—social, mobile, or big data experts—find themselves interacting with consumers and customers more frequently and intimately than traditional customer-facing departments. Consumers are demanding that these experts solve their problems and provide the latest information about products and services.

Unfortunately, these specialized practitioners often lack the knowledge and skills to do so. As a result, customers become increasingly dissatisfied, complaints mount, and management becomes aware that this segregated approach is causing larger problems for the organization.

When encountering this problem, most business leaders do one of two things. First, they pour more money, time, and resources into these segregated digital initiatives in an attempt to solve the problem. Or second, they seek to reinvent their organizations as highly social, highly mobile, and big-data–friendly; they see the problem as part of a much larger issue and use it as a catalyst to reinvent the company with a new and "improved" structure and substance. Both of these approaches are doomed to failure because they only serve to further fragment the organization. Reinvention erodes the unique identity and value proposition upon which the company was built.

Consider a third option. All business leaders want results. They've spent the money and assigned the resources necessary to build large social communities, develop mobile applications, and collect massive amounts of data. They've done the work to become more sophisticated in how they manage and use these digital initiatives. But they want these initiatives to generate traditional business results: increased revenue and profit, reduced expense, and improved performance. They want these digital initiatives to translate into bottom-line results, such as more customers, higher conversion rates, increased customer lifetime value, new markets, and greater opportunities.

This book is designed to help you achieve these results within your own organization—to help organizations both big and small become a Big Social Mobile enterprise.

Big Social Mobile is not about the standard list of topics these digital initiatives bring to mind—increasing your company's friends and followers, designing the coolest mobile application, and collecting more big data. Rather, it is built upon the premise that these three major digital initiatives—big data, social media, and mobile technology—have the potential to radically improve business performance, if they are implemented in a way that enhances and supports what has traditionally made a business unique and profitable—if they are integrated into each other and into the goals, objectives, people, processes, technology, and information of the organization itself.

Big Social Mobile takes a position that strikes me as firmly grounded in traditional business principles, but it is one that others might find radical. It holds that business has not changed despite all of these technological advances, and neither has the way organizational success is measured. What has changed is how you must play the game, how technology and methodology must be blended together, one enabling the other, all filtered through the perspective of how an organization can—and must—adapt to meet the evolving demands of a new social consumer in a new social economy.

On the journey to become Big Social Mobile, organizations do not start from ground zero. Most already have initiatives in place. Employees strive within them to succeed; managers seek to achieve goals, become more effective and efficient, and satisfy customer and consumer demands. But these fine efforts also pull the enterprise apart because they are segregated from the organization's core culture, philosophy, value proposition, and beliefs. Huge amounts of money are invested to develop new mobile applications or to increase the company's social community, cool technology and more followers are the only results. There is little impact on revenue and a negative impact on profit.

As each of these segregated initiatives grows in complexity, it becomes an iceberg, where only the smallest amount of the problem it is creating is visible to business leaders. On the surface, the segregated initiatives seem to meet their objectives—they attract followers, increase engagement and usage, and produce more data—but in this segregated state they are not creating real growth. They produce an increase in complexity and cost without a resulting increase in profit. It is unsustainable. Only through better integration will organizations overcome the larger obstacles that these segregated initiatives represent.

In the first section of this book I'll begin by exploring the problems these initiatives cause when organizations adopt a segregated mind-set and how an integrated approach can solve these problems. Using examples that illustrate the benefits of the latter and the perils of the former, I'll describe organizations that have grappled with the same issues your organization is facing. As you proceed deeper into the book, you will see how to shift your thinking, setting aside the common lens through which social media, mobile technology, and big data experts see these digital initiatives and instead see them from a traditional business perspective—how they can, and should, create tangible business results. From this new perspective, you will understand how you don't have to reinvent your organization to achieve these new objectives but simply integrate these initiatives into the core of your organization itself.

The middle section of the book defines a methodology that my clients have adopted to achieve ambitious business objectives. From analyzing digital relationships to identifying ideal digital behaviors, I'll provide specific steps and advice that organizations can follow to become Big Social Mobile. The final chapters examine three issues that will arise as organizations attempt to adopt an integrated mind-set—the challenge that consumer-controlled mobile technology presents, the need to demystify big data, and the importance of anticipating the impact of new technology on the future.

I've written this book in a way that will be relevant to a wide range of business readers. It addresses topics that should resonate with executives who have a deep understanding of business as well as with specialized practitioners of big data, social media, and mobile technology who possess a deep understanding of their specialty.

I've also written it with a firm belief that though these initiatives have not changed business itself, the audience for these initiatives has changed. Consumers now have more power than ever before, and for organizations to take back power in this corporate-consumer relationship, they must discover how to reshape themselves without reinvention. They must change the way they think about these initiatives without losing sight of what makes them unique, and valuable. An integrated mind-set is the key to this improved approach.

Unfortunately, few companies have yet to become effective at integrating these digital initiatives into their enterprise, creating a seamless experience for customers and consumers across both the physical and digital landscape, merging the multiple spheres that online consumers exist within, and creating tangible business results.

Therein lies the opportunity. By reshaping your organization into a Big Social Mobile enterprise you can seize that opportunity. This book will explain why doing so is critical and how do to it.

Part I

SEEING AND THINKING BIG PICTURE

THE NEW SOCIAL ECONOMY HAS NOT changed how success in business is measured but rather how success is achieved.

Chapter 1

THE INTEGRATED ENTERPRISE

JUST ABOUT EVERY MAJOR ORGANIZATION AROUND the world has invested heavily in three key digital initiatives—social media, mobile technology, and big data—in recent years. This investment has been in dollars and in people. Companies have recruited specialized practitioners for each of these digital initiatives, adopted new technology, and hired third-party specialists. They have a lot riding on the success of these initiatives.

Executives have been told they must re-invent themselves as highly social or highly mobile or big data-friendly; some say the sustainability of their enterprise is at stake, that these digital initiatives have revolutionized business. Big, social, and mobile are on all leaders' minds, and they're looking for results.

At first glance it may seem as if these efforts have paid off. Most organizations have seen huge percentage increases in friends, fans, and followers on a wide array of social platforms. A majority of larger organizations have launched mobile applications that are state-of-the-art, highly downloaded, and praised as user-friendly. They revel in the volumes of data they've generated or collected, proclaiming that they now know more about consumers—website visitors, social media followers, and mobile users—than ever before. And these things are all true.

But look below the surface of these results. They represent narrowly defined gains in separate, highly specialized areas and not much else. How have digital initiatives helped companies achieve traditional business goals: increasing revenue, reducing expenses, and improving profit? Has this new, greater understanding of or improved relationships with customers or consumers led to these tangible measures of value or the things that directly drive them? Have they helped businesses evolve so that they are better suited to operate in a global, digital world, where consumers inhabit both a physical and digital landscape?

The answer to these questions is a resounding "no." Certainly the potential is there for social media, mobile technology, and big data to achieve these objectives. But that's never going to happen as long as organizations continue to launch these initiatives in a segregated manner—segregated from each other and from the larger organization itself, its mission, and its objectives. As long as the emphasis is on boosting the number of friends and followers, creating ever more technically sophisticated mobile applications, or collecting increasingly greater amounts of data, these initiatives will have a minimal impact on the true measures of organizational performance.

If, on the other hand, these initiatives are integrated into the enterprise itself, woven together and into its people, processes, technology, and information, they can drive results that build upon and enhance the company's differentiators and value propositions, properly position them to connect with today's social consumer, and compete in a diverse new social economy, adding real, tangible value. When integrated properly, these initiatives can yield the results that executives are seeking and can turn any organization, both big and small, into a Big Social Mobile enterprise.

BIG SOCIAL MOBILE VERSUS THE TRADITIONAL ENTERPRISE

The differences between Big Social Mobile enterprises and ones that separate and isolate these digital initiatives are numerous and multifaceted. It's not just a matter of actions but attitudes. Leaders within integrated enterprises, for instance, have a very different perspective on these three initiatives. These leaders esteem the traditional measures of organizational performance and the value proposition that made them successful and yet understand that social media, mobile technology, and big data are strategic initiatives that must be blended together and integrated into every aspect of their organization. They are constantly questioning and talking about how these initiatives contribute to major business objectives and the supporting goals of each department.

They are actively and continuously involved in decisions that impact these initiatives.

In organizations that handle big, social, and mobile in the traditional, segregated manner, leaders often have little awareness of or involvement in these initiatives; each initiative is run by a separate, specialized subject-matter expert. Since executives do not focus upon them, their success is measured in terms that these specialized practitioners define as success: more friends or followers, more downloads, or more data.

Here are the traits that differentiate an integrated from a segregated organization:

THE SEGREGATED APPROACH—SEE FIGURE 1.1

- Runs isolated projects in each of the three areas. Marketing or digital marketing manages social media with a low-level marketer/analyst in charge; the Information Technology (IT) group manages mobile with the help of an outsourced third-party developer; and IT manages the consolidation of big data.
- Fails to tie initiatives to corporate goals. Social media objectives focus on numerical measurements of followership, engagement, and sentiment; mobile objectives relate to the number of downloads and usage metrics; big data efforts concentrate on the amount of data collected.
- Creates self-contained initiatives that aren't woven into core processes. Traditional enterprise functions, processes, technology, and information outside of the three digital initiatives are disconnected from these initiatives; marketing promotions are not integrated with digital marketing efforts; sales opportunities arising in these areas are not handled by Sales; customer issues are not handled by Customer Service; and big-data-related information is not utilized for planning and decision making. The customer experience is inconsistent across mediums and channels.
- Lacks executive oversight of these initiatives. Corporate leaders see big, social, and mobile as supporting efforts that should be run by subject-matter experts.
- Does not tie social and mobile data (big data) to traditional enterprise data. Customers are unique within each data set and cannot be identified

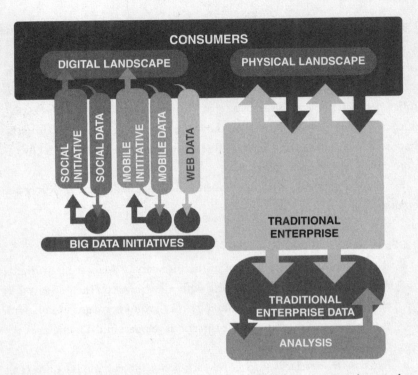

Figure 1.1 The segregated approach to digital initiatives, leaving them isolated from core, traditional enterprise functions.

across each of these different digital spheres or across both the physical and digital landscape.

- Looks at information as a nonstrategic asset of the organization. Perceives information to be relative to each initiative and separate from core processes and enterprise information.

THE INTEGRATED APPROACH—SEE FIGURE 1.2

- Measures the success of digital initiatives using traditional metrics such as revenue, expense, and profit and their ability to influence these, while also measuring elements unique to each initiative (number of fans, engagement, downloads, video views, etc.)
- Seeks to create a similar customer experience across both the traditional and digital landscapes, through all channels, creating processes

to standardize this experience. Uses this standardization to create internal efficiencies, improve customer and consumer satisfaction, and increase brand loyalty.

- Views digital initiatives as directly impacting the company's long-term success; information generated by big data is used to gain a strategic advantage, improve performance, and is used by every function within the enterprise; big data and traditional data are merged into one data set.

- Embeds digital initiatives into core enterprise processes, with subject-matter experts owning only the technology and processes specific to each initiative; subject-matter experts facilitate enterprise-wide involvement.

- Encourages department and functional leaders to be socially aware; digital initiatives are integrated into departmental planning, and this information is combined with traditional enterprise information.

- Disperses social media, mobile technology, and big data information throughout the enterprise; the enterprise runs active processes that seek to bridge the gap between enterprise and big data so that customers are uniquely identified and so that behavior can be analyzed using new techniques and can be leveraged with new marketing and sales techniques.

- Makes sure the owners of digital initiatives articulate and disseminate their vision for how their efforts will support the company's core value proposition and drive traditional profit-oriented results.

* * *

In looking at these traits, be aware that most organizations are not all one or the other. Few companies have achieved the ideal, fully integrated approach, and a dwindling number of organizations remain saddled with a completely segregated model. The goal of today's executive should be to apply consistent and persistent pressure that helps their organization evolve to become a Big Social Mobile enterprise. This means breaking down the barriers that exist between each of these initiatives. It also requires tearing down the fences between these new specialties and the traditional enterprise processes and policies.

But this does not mean that the organization must be reinvented, magically transformed into something different, web-based, highly social, or purely

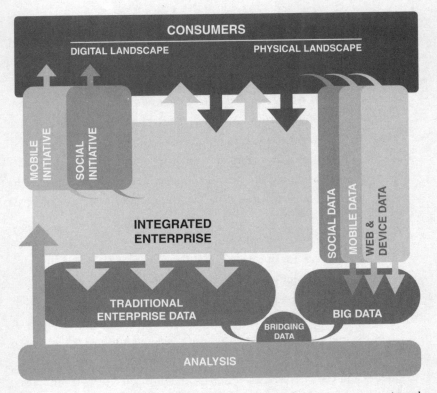

Figure 1.2   The integrated enterprise, where each digital initiative is woven into the people, process, technology, and information of traditional enterprise functions.

mobile. Executives cannot allow the organization to lose sight of what made their company what it is and the value proposition upon which it is based. These traditional drivers of success are the stakes in the ground upon which everything big, social, and mobile must be tied. Despite the constant hype associated with these digital initiatives, the basic rules of business have not changed.

ONE COMPANY'S JOURNEY TO BECOME BIG SOCIAL MOBILE

For a large photography and imaging consumer goods company, the journey to become Big Social Mobile started with a simple question: What rebate amounts would prompt consumers to buy their products? Carl, the Chief Marketing Officer (CMO), was relying on historical information that varied discounts by geographic market and product. The results were highly influenced by retailer strategies, local economics, seasonality, and supply chain performance.

Carl knew that the company's social and mobile initiatives might provide a different answer. His company had approximately 40,000 fans within their social media communities; an unimpressive number. But their largest retailer possessed a 7-million-member social community and was always eager to partner on promotions. Carl gave the green light to begin testing rebate amounts on their social community. Once it began, other retailers got wind of it and requested the same promotional programs. Carl was able to widen the tests, and his company's social community quickly began to grow.

After the test had run for two months, Carl had sufficient data to answer the original question. And the information was specific; the CMO could now see the relationship between different rebate amounts and consumer demand. He deduced he could use these social communities to test new rebate price levels, even combining them with different promotions and marketing language to quickly see their impact on consumer behavior—something impossible with the traditional approach.

But in the course of doing so, Carl discovered that his company had no way of comparing data about online consumers who took advantage of the rebates to the customers in the company database. In addition, the data on the 80,000 users who downloaded his company's third-party-developed mobile app were also completely separated from his traditional customer and social media data. Thus, customers had multiple, separate identities—the traditional data identified them by product registration or sales order numbers; the social media and mobile apps identified them by email address, user IDs, or mobile numbers. His company's big data initiative didn't tie these different identities together or uniquely identify their customers or consumers.

Even more alarming, the silos went beyond the data. No one in the Customer Service department was tracking, comparing, or responding effectively to issues raised by social media and mobile customers; no one in Product Development was tracking product improvement suggestions that came through social media; Sales was uninvolved when a customer was looking for an upgrade or a consumer showed interest in a new product; and no one was comparing the behavior of consumers online to consumer behavior in physical stores.

Carl began implementing a series of changes in response to these disconnects, including:

- Fostering executive involvement in all social and mobile initiatives so that they were tied directly to the achievement of corporate goals.
- Changing the focus of the company's big data initiative so that it brought together all data—traditional enterprise, social, and mobile data—in a way that not only showed larger trends, but also identified specific customers.
- Introducing new types of analyses that tied consumer demographics to behavioral patterns so that functional department heads could integrate information into their processes and decision making.
- Modifying the existing Customer Service technology and processes to ensure that Agents received information about customers from both their traditional enterprise applications and social and mobile platforms so that they could respond to inquiries more effectively.

Mobile was a bigger problem; since the company's primary products were cameras, smart phones, with their built-in cameras, were actually preventing growth of core product lines. Product Development was paired with Social Media to solicit suggestions from consumers for the company's new line of "social products." The company also fought back by changing its mobile app to embed discounted instant printing, to promote the functionality of higher-grade cameras, and to push discounts directly to consumers likely to upgrade at holidays or when big data revealed they were planning a vacation. Videos and articles were designed to highlight what could be done with real cameras that couldn't be done with smart phones.

With these and other efforts, Carl put the company in a much better position to determine which customers represented the greatest opportunity and then use this information to target these customers with specific marketing techniques. They also were able to learn which customers were likely to need new supplies and at what times of year, allowing them to capture these customers with advertisements, discounts, and seasonal promotions. Carl was also able to leverage the integrated enterprise and big data to change how the company marketed, adopting a *micro-marketing* technique—targeting small and specific consumer groups with messages that were designed to have a higher sales success rate.

Perhaps the most significant change, though, was that every function and leadership level in the company became involved in social, mobile, and big data initiatives. Wider distribution of the information pulled from big data and process changes made social and mobile efforts meaningful to each functional department; social and mobile consumers became just as tangible to employees as customers who called on phones or sent emails.

While Carl's company is still in the early stages of becoming a Big Social Mobile enterprise, it has already reaped significant, tangible benefits from their new approach, ranging from increased sales to improved long-term product development strategies. Finding specific areas where big data, social, and mobile initiatives could be directly tied to the entire enterprise removed the confusion caused by the increased complexity these initiatives represent. This complexity often overwhelms executives—and entire organizations. When this happens, they adopt an approach that is easy to understand—one focused on specific, simple goals like increasing followers or engagement, building a better mobile app, or collecting more data. However, as we have seen, these goals are often contrary to the overarching goals of the enterprise.

THE CHALLENGE OF COMPLEXITY

As businesses grow, they often become too complex for the current leadership, processes, and systems to control. An increase in the number of customers creates the need for additional personnel; higher transactional volume requires better technology to process requests; additional products creates the need for additional product developers, warehouse workers, warehouse space, and assets. New business channels, in a potentially global market, can give rise to issues ranging from problematic legal requirements to excessively complex supply chains. Emerging technologies that fuel growth are quickly trumped by even better emerging technologies. Leaders scramble to keep pace and make difficult decisions in the gray area between right and wrong.

To meet this increase in complexity caused by growth, companies add people, processes, and technology. Management of the business becomes dispersed among a new group of leaders and employees who are increasingly grounded in functional specialties: Sales, Marketing, Operations, Information Technology, Finance, Accounting. But at the same time, the core value proposition of the business—what customers find valuable about that business—changes very little. In addition, the new managers who are now responsible for communicating this value proposition to prospects, delivering it to customers, and disseminating it through various mediums are one step removed from the original idea upon which that business was built, the one that intrigued or convinced consumers. Being specialized and one step removed from the core of the business, these new managers and practitioners show an increased tendency to focus solely on their area of expertise. They attempt to think holistically, but their perspective, the goals they set, and the results they strive for are influenced by their previous experience and expertise.

While specialization in the face of growth helps companies navigate complex new issues and problems, it has negative side effects. Companies must invest tremendous amounts of time and energy trying to control how products and services are positioned, sold, and delivered across new channels and new territories. The core strategy that made the company unique often suffers while the company struggles to understand and adapt to its position in a changing marketplace. Specialized managers and new employees skew the corporate perspective and pull energy into localized initiatives that detract from what the business was actually put there to do—generate profit. It's not that corporate leaders intentionally commit these mistakes, but that the complexity caused by growth causes people to become focused on narrow goals that contribute little or not at all to larger business objectives.

And this is only the complexity that comes from growth—the need to do the same things at an increased volume and velocity.

Add social media, mobile technology, and big data, and things become exponentially more complex. Social media has performed the wholesale renovation of branding and marketing techniques and has created a fundamental shift in the *corporate-consumer relationship*; mobile technology has mainstreamed a brand-new platform of disparate devices completely controlled by a changing consumer; big data has introduced a much larger volume of data and information fragmented across a broader digital landscape.

To meet these new challenges, leaders add new, increasingly specialized practicioners: digital marketers to manage social media, mobile developers to create mobile apps, and information technologists and analysts to handle big data. Management of the organization is again further dispersed.

As you might imagine—as you've probably experienced—things become lost in this translation. No matter how much executives try to educate themselves, social media, mobile technology, and big data are foreign concepts.

The existing systems and processes that these leaders became familiar with over the years clashes with the demands of operating in a digital world. This digital landscape is too far removed from the center of the corporate enterprise, and the skills required to operate effectively there are too specialized and too new. Leaders need subject-matter experts—big data, social, and mobile practitioners—who possess very different skills and backgrounds and perspectives than they're used to.

While leaders don't give carte blanche to these experts, they are much more likely to give them more freedom to control their areas than they accord to other functional managers in disciplines that are familiar to them, such as Finance, Operations, and Sales. They do not question engineers on design specification, developers on proprietary algorithms, or the graphic designers on layout techniques, and so they also don't question these new specialized practitioners. They allow these experts to operate as free-standing entities within their enterprise.

Have you ever walked into the engineering wing of a corporate headquarters, the cubicle world of developers, or the open air office of graphics artists and felt that you have entered another world, one far removed from the larger corporate culture that employs them? They look and feel different from the rest of the company. These groups, with their own independent people, processes and technology, take on a life and culture of their own, one that is far removed from the strict value proposition that appeals to the customers. The offices of social media marketers, mobile developers, and big data analysts often feel the same; they too are subject-matter experts in charge of knowledge that seems esoteric or at least unfamiliar.

Organizational leaders do not manage these specialized areas in the same hands-on fashion they do core areas of their business, justifying this looser approach because they lack the expertise to be as involved as they normally are. In addition, experts tend to operate at the fringes of the enterprise, far removed from direct interaction with customers. Leaders and mainstream managers act as buffers between these independently operating experts and the consumer.

What's different about social media, mobile technology, and big data—and what makes the situation more complex—is that each of these functions are actually on the front line of customer interactions. Within their separate silos, these three areas see, understand, and deal with consumers through a never-ending feed of information, one that is far more intimate than the periodic interactions managers and employees within the Sales, Customer Service, or

Account Management departments have with customers. Enmeshed in their own specialized functions, the purveyors of these digital initiatives aren't posting content, designing applications, or managing data in a way that relates their effort to the larger corporate strategy; the complexity of their work and their tasks insulate them from corporate goals in the same way that product designers aren't held accountable for the revenue their products eventually generate.

This lack of accountability and integration these digital initiatives have with the core of businesses must change. Complexity is an obstacle but should not be an excuse. Organizations need a process that pushes them past the complex issues they're facing in order to access the valuable information these specialists possess—information that Big Social Mobile enterprises use to great competitive advantage.

THE TRANSFORMATIVE POWER OF DISTRIBUTED INFORMATION

On the surface, the manner in which many organizations deal with information generated from their social media and mobile technology efforts makes sense. They analyze social media data for how effectively consumers respond to company posts or how actively they engage with the brand. Mobile data provide insights into how effectively customers are adopting the mobile application, and how frequently they use it. This information helps social and mobile practitioners improve consumer engagement and sentiment, something that will benefit the company in the long run.

High-performing companies have learned how to shatter these silos within their organization, encouraging and even forcing one function to interact and share information with another. Research and Development launches a new product, Marketing promotes it, Sales sells it, and Operations delivers or implements it. And then Operations feeds back to Research and Development information that drives product improvement and highlights to Sales and Marketing what customers find most valuable, and how they are using the product in ways the company never anticipated. As a result, the focus of marketing materials and sales presentations improves to resonate more deeply with new prospects (see Figure 1.3).

Big Social Mobile enterprises understand the value of using information in a similar manner. They analyze posted content and solicit information based on corporate needs: they determine what consumers love and hate about their

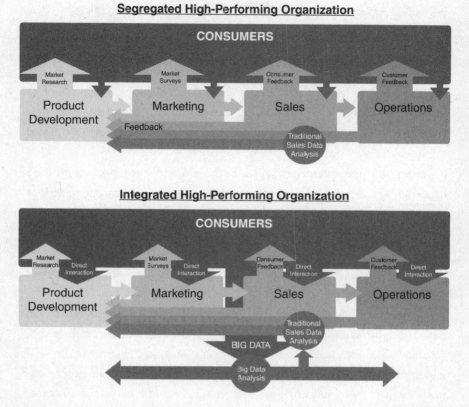

Figure 1.3   The difference between how segregated and integrated high-performing organizations interact with the market and share information between departments to increase learning and effectiveness. Integrated enterprises have more direct interaction, leverage big data, and combine big data with traditional enterprise data for greater insight.

brand; they assess how this love or hate impacts consumer sentiment; they examine what products or services consumer value most, and where they stack up versus competitors; they figure out what marketing campaigns resonate most deeply and how and when these campaigns convert prospects to customers. They analyze the nuance of consumer behavior relative to every interaction they so that they can employ more effective techniques. They use information for more than just increasing followers, engagement, and improving sentiment.

And Big Social Mobile enterprises capitalize on the information in even more impactful ways. Not only do they use it to understand consumers, the marketplace, and trends from a broad perspective, they are able to extract individual opportunities from the data—specific prospects to pursue, specific problems to solve, specific people to solicit, specific new groups that could potentially become customers. And they put all of this information directly into the hands of those employees that can put it to the best use, at exactly the right time. Information is not retained with isolated initiative silos, but distributed across the organization so that not only is the entire enterprise socially aware, but each function is able to leverage the results of these digital initiatives.

As a result, the enterprise realizes both hard and soft returns from their digital initiatives, while at the same time allowing the consumer to benefit as well. Consumers are now interacting with the employee who can add the most value to the conversation or solve the problem quickest—something that is vitally important to and builds brand loyalty with today's social consumer—and they are getting a consistent experience regardless of whom they interact with, across any medium.

Big Social Mobile enterprises also actively break down the barriers between data and information silos. Most companies keep traditional customer data separated from social and mobile data, but fully integrated enterprises tie social and mobile customer data to the traditional data that reside within other databases, such as those that support customer service, order entry, and customer relationship management. This integration of traditional enterprise information and big data allows the company to understand and target consumers more effectively. These information-savvy organizations don't distinguish between traditional customer interactions and ones that occur digitally; they extract, compare, and use data from both.

Information, then, is the driver of an integrated approach. Big Social Mobile enterprises do not expend significant resources to manage big data for big data's sake, but for competitive advantage. They recognize that the rise of social media and mobile technology presents them with opportunities that go far beyond improved engagement and they understand that they can make their overall business more successful—by integrating big, social, and mobile into the enterprise.

REDEFINING SUCCESS

To create a Big Social Mobile enterprise—one that uses new technology and techniques but is driven and united by traditional organizational objectives—organizations need to redefine what success is for these three digital initiatives. Until they are defined in terms that relate them to the broader enterprise, they will continue to measure themselves based upon metrics that are commonly used by their peer group of fellow practitioners.

This redefinition requires a change in perception. While big data, social, and mobile initiatives may look like other specialized efforts, they are actually quite different. Management, however, tries to classify them using traditional labels: social media as a new marketing technique; mobile development as a technology effort; big data as analytics. The use of traditional labels isolates and minimizes the impact of digital initiatives.

A social media practitioner is hired and creates a presence on Facebook, Twitter, YouTube, LinkedIn, and other social media platforms. This digital marketer sets about attracting a base of friends, fans, and followers. They incorporate marketing materials into their efforts and borrow content from press releases and brochures. Their initial measure of success involves the number of followers generated, and as their initiative progresses they focus on consumer engagement and sometimes sentiment. Some companies generate more followers than others, or more engagement than others, but generally, an effort is considered successful if the number of followers and degree of engagement increase over time.

Consider, though, that the digital marketer is interacting with followers who might never learn about the actual value proposition the company was built upon and might never buy the company's products or services. The initiative is operating within a vacuum. It is led by a social media practitioner whose expertise lies in posting content and managing online communites; someone who has been taught to borrow content from wherever they can find it in hopes of attracting more and more friends, fans, and followers.

This initiative is doing little to communicate the brand's message or its differentiators; it is doing nothing to generate profit. But it is generating considerable expense.

At the same time another initiative is under way within the enterprise. Mobile developers have been hired, or outsourced, and a mobile app has been created and launched. It is deemed a success if it offers consumers a way to find the company, see its goods and services, and allows customers to reach Customer Service Agents via phone, email, or chat when necessary. But it, too, is generating expense and doing little to create profit or further the corporate mission.

As these social and mobile initiatives grow they are creating data—a lot of data—and another initiative is launched, one that seeks to gather, consolidate and interpret this data. It is being run by the company's internal IT staff and requires entirely new applications and infrastructure completely separate from the enterprise's traditional technology infrastructure. Its purpose is to interpret what is happening as a result of the social and mobile initiatives and provide management with information they can use. It is considered a success if it produces evidence that friends and followers are increasing, provides demographic information these followers and demonstrates that their apps are being used. This initiative, too, generates significant expense and no profit, and it too operates without being tied in to larger corporate objectives.

These criteria for success are understandable if not acceptable. They can be justified because today every company believes they must have a social and mobile presence, and deal with the resulting data. But these initiatives are not successful when viewed from an enterprise perspective, the traditional perspective that executives must maintain when executing against the basic profit-oriented or value-based mission of every organization.

For years, companies have relied on clearly defined sales processes to drive their businesses. Sales might be retail workers behind a counter, cold callers from an overseas third-party call center, or traditional sales people that knock on doors and ask for business. Some companies rely more on sales promotions, others on brand-building advertising—but all are designed to turn consumers into customers.

Operations, in turn, followed Sales to satisfy the commitment made to the customer during the sales process. Operational processes and departments varied widely by industry and by company. But regardless of the simplicity or complexity of operational processes, or the inclusion or exclusion of departments such as customer service, order processing, warehousing pick/pack, retail, or delivery operations, companies satisfy their customers through these operational processes.

Sales and Operations have traditionally been the core of companies because they satisfy the main purpose of all companies: generating customers and satisfying their needs. This does not mean that other areas of the business do not also have the ability to win or lose customers, but that a company must have efficient Sales and Operations to remain viable for any significant period of time. And because they are the core of business, Sales and Operations share the same performance metrics used by the business itself. Sales is measured by revenue generated and Operations is measured by the expense generated while delivering products or services. When combined they create the basic profit equation.

Other departments—Marketing, Finance, Product Development, Information Technology—are measured based upon these secondary measures which show their ability to help Sales and Operations achieve the core company objectives. These departments must manage their expenses like all departments, but they are not held to the same standard. It is the unwritten rule of business: those who directly interact with the customer, those who generate them, deliver products and services to them, and then keep them happy, turning them into repeat customers driving long-term customer value, are most accountable.

Social media and mobile technology are changing this. Many customers now use social media as their first touch point to investigate a brand, to see if they feel any connection to its image, and to determine whether their friends and family are familiar with its products or services. If these social consumers decide to become customers or experience a problem, social media is often the first place they return to. They reflexively go back to their first point of interaction with that company. New social consumers also check to see whether the company has a mobile application. If it does, it often becomes the first place they go when they need to interact with the company for any reason: product problem, add-on products or services, or to repurchase. Mobile technology, like social media, has become deeply embedded in both the Sales and Operations processes.

Social and mobile initiatives are measured as if they are supporting functions when in fact today's social consumer has turned them into core business functions.

The highly specialized employees working within social and mobile initiatives lack the knowledge and skills to perform these Sales and Operations functions. They have no experience or training in upselling customers and maximizing revenue per sale or customer lifetime value. Moreover, these specialized employees often aren't astute about brand messages or the larger goals of the company. They may communicate with the customer in a way that commoditizes a product or service or that emphasizes speed of delivery instead of quality. As skilled as these specialists are at increasing engagement, the segmented environment they work within does not equip them with the tools they need to function as extensions of Sales or Operations..

The company could attempt to reinvent itself, putting even more resources into social and mobile programs. But in doing this it would dilute what made the company unique and successful to begin with. The answer then is to integrate these functions back into the enterprise so that the employees who understand how to maximize interactions with the consumer are there during critical moments: generating leads, closing business, servicing customers, gathering key information. To do this the company must have processes in place that ensure customers can interact with the employees who are best suited to respond to their issue—just as businesses have done long before this digital revolution.

Organizations can determine whether they've redefined success in an integrative manner based on how they answer questions such as the following:

- How often do highly engaged consumers become customers or make repeat purchases?
- What is the conversation rate of social consumers to customers compared to the company's traditional conversion rate? How does this compare to consumers registered on a company mobile app?
- Do highly engaged, social consumers have a higher lifetime value than traditional customers, and which are more easily influenced?
- What is the actual volume of leads coming from the social and mobile channel?
- What percentage of existing customers are downloading mobile applications and how much more efficient are these apps making interactive processes? How much is the company saving as a result?

Companies can also measure whether they've redefined success by asking questions related to their strategic objectives:

- How many product improvements came from social and mobile channels?
- What does the competitive landscape look like from the consumers' perspective?
- How many product upgrade inquiries have come as a result of content posted on social platforms?

- How have social platforms extended the reach of the organization, opened new market segments, or identified highly profitable subsegments of existing markets?
- How has social media or mobile technology increased brand recognition, and has this increase resulted in tangible sales opportunities?
- How realistic is the organization's long-term strategy considering the new social consumers' attitudes and behaviors?

As organizations attempt to transition from a segregated to an integrated approach, they should monitor how they're answering these questions. Over time, they will find their answers changing, and they can chart their progress toward an integrated ideal by the shift in their responses. The easier they find it to answer these questions, the more progress they're making.

Now let's turn to another litmus test that measures an organization's progress toward becoming a Big Social Mobile enterprise: the mobile application.

AN APP FOR THE AGES

You can often tell a Big Social Mobile enterprise by its mobile app. Too often, companies create technologically advanced apps that have little to do with their overall mission or strategy. Starbucks became 2012's most dominant player in the $500-million mobile wallet market with a deceptively simple app that fits perfectly with their overall strategy.[1] When Starbucks began their rapid expansion in the late 1980s, they did so with a marketing campaign that positioned their coffee shops as destinations where coffee lovers could get more than just the best coffee in the world. Their stores were what they called people's "third place," the place people went when they wanted to get away from home or work—a home away from home. And the company meant it. They created spacious, stylized store layouts in areas that were often the most expensive real estate in urban areas. They were one of the first chains to offer free wi-fi. This approach, combined with the quality of their coffee and American's interest in the new sophisticated coffee craze Starbucks created, drove growth that at its peak allowed them to open an average of two stores per day for nearly a decade.

Starbucks became more than just a brand. It became a lifestyle brand, something never before done in the coffee industry; something people would have said was impossible. Its success was built upon customer loyalty and a long-term view of customer value. Making the buying experience as rich and rewarding for the consumer as possible became natural objectives of that strategy.

The Starbucks mobile application was launched in 2011 and initially mirrored their highly successful customer gift card program—a program that led to one in ten US adults receiving a Starbucks gift card during the fourth quarter of 2012, a quarter when more than $1 billion was loaded onto those cards.[2] At a time when other companies were developing apps that had as many bells and whistles as could be conceivably added, Starbucks' mobile app was noticeably low-tech. It could do little more than load the digital gift cards and subtract money at the point-of-sale. But this was enough. Consumers flocked to the app and made it the only highly adopted, fully utilized digital wallet app on the market for the next five years. No other mobile wallet or payment system has even come close to its success.

To some it seemed that Starbucks was taking the easy way out with a barebones app that did nothing more than facilitate a sales transaction. But what Starbucks actually did was tremendously difficult—they ignored the advice of typical mobile developers and what was considered best practices at the time. Starbucks focused on harmonizing the app with their core value proposition— not coffee, or not just coffee—but the experience that their most loyal customers loved about the retail experience and what could make it even better.

This experience has to do with the sheer volume of orders they execute on a daily basis—approximately 10.5 billion cups of coffee per day, in North America alone.[3] With a total of 87,000 possible drink combinations, this volume could easily bring nearly any process to a halt, leading to frustrated customers and a high percentage of abandoned sales.[4] Yet despite this volume, the average time from a consumer entering the line to receiving their drink is well under three minutes, and declining. Starbucks redesigned ice scoopers in order to shave a mere 14 seconds off of iced drink preparation time and accepted credit card orders of under $25 without signatures—the part of the purchasing process that takes the longest time.[5] The customer sales ordering and fulfillment processes are as highly engineered as the most complicated drink recipe on the menu.

The mobile app reduced the payment portion of the ordering process to less than one second for more than 20 percent of orders, it represents a significant cost savings for Starbucks and a significant improvement in the overall Starbucks experience for customers each time they visit. The app is still one of the most downloaded apps each week.[6]

Starbucks shows what is possible when a company remains true to its core value proposition and accepts that social and mobile must be embedded into the core processes that deliver this value to their customers. For Starbucks, social and mobile had to make the customer experience better, reinforcing the corporate focus on customer lifetime value, while at the same time driving revenue or reducing expense. The Starbucks mobile app does this, and more.

A key driver of the success of the Starbucks app is that it rewards the most loyal customers with a free drink after a preset number of visits. This encourages consumers to mentally engage with the app and work toward achieving the goal—what is often called "gamification." The loyalty program does drive adoption and usage, but more importantly it drives the average number of visits per customer and therefore improves customer lifetime value. Starbucks could have used a different incentive program. They could have used the most common reward program: spend a certain amount and get a percentage discount. But Starbucks didn't. Their program is driven by number of visits, regardless of the amount spent. This approach and these performance measures support Starbucks strategic focus on the long-term relationship with customers.

How did Starbucks know the exact number of drinks that would trigger an improvement in customer visits? They used the big data generated by their mobile app to understand customer behavior, and then manipulated the Sales and Operations processes until they found the optimal solution—optimal meaning it maximized revenue and customer experience. Social media, mobile technology, and big data all tightly integrated with each other and integrated the corporate objectives to create a Big Social Mobile enterprise.

Starbucks received tremendous benefits from an app that reflected the Big Social Mobile principles of integration. In the next chapter, we will examine the range of benefits organizations receive when they convert to this thinking.

Chapter 2

BOTTOM LINE, MISSION-CRITICAL BENEFITS

FOR MANY EXECUTIVES, THE BENEFITS OF SOCIAL MEDIA, mobile technology, and big data have been amorphous—they know that they must engage in these activities but they're not sure how to monetize the results. They may add 100,000 followers, see thousands of people downloading their mobile application, or collect servers full of data, but translating any of this into something that will directly drive business results seems impossible.

While collecting followers, downloads, and data are all important, they will produce limited tangible benefits because they reflect a segregated mind-set. When big data, social media, and mobile technology initiatives are linked to each other and the organizational mission, benefits that are both more specific and more wide-ranging can be realized. Specifically, organizations can expect the following positive outcomes:

- Identifying and gaining consumers more cost-effectively
- Facilitating micro-marketing to improve conversation rates
- Uncovering new potential customer markets
- Improving consumer targeting to reduced costs
- Leveraging followers to sell and improve products and services, and processes

- Improving customer satisfaction
- Shaping consumer behavior into more profitable patterns

We'll look at each of these benefits individually, but first let's focus on a company that has realized a wide range of positive results because of its successful integration of digital inititatives into its organizational strategy: Dunkin' Donuts.

SOCIAL MEDIA GOES STRATEGIC

As we saw in the previous chapter, Starbucks benefited from its integrated approach, using mobile technology to reinforce its value proposition and strategic objectives. But this is only one of many ways companies can benefit from their digital initiatives. Big Social Mobile enterprises can solve a variety of problems and take advantage of many opportunities.

Compare how Starbucks' main rival, Dunkin' Donuts, took advantage of an integrated strategy. While Dunkin' Donuts was late to utilize mobile technology, it was one of the first brands to create a strong, cohesive social media program. Like many companies using social media, Dunkin' Donuts first built a large base of followers and then focused on consumer engagement. Once this was achieved, it went significantly beyond these common initial objectives. Kevin Vine, interactive marketing manager at Dunkin' Donuts, describes the company's ambitious objectives: "Our social media strategy is aimed at growing and maintaining a highly engaged global community of Dunkin' Donuts fans. We work to consistently provide meaningful content and promote a two-way dialogue between the brand and our passionate fans."[1]

How, then, does a social media strategy provide broader benefits when its primary goal appears to be increased engagement?

Dunkin' Donuts integrated social media into its strategic planning process; it intended to use social media to meet the objective of improving brand loyalty, something that had a very direct impact upon its bottom line, by increasing the number of times each customer visited one of their stores. Their approach enlisted regional partners to hyperlocalize social media efforts, connecting with local communities and therefore building loyalty to the overarching brand through these highly personalized interactions. This personalized connection directly appeals to today's social consumer, who is willing to make purchasing decisions based upon this connection.

At the same time that Dunkin' Donuts was directly appealing to highly social consumers, they were also using social media to pull traditional customers—those who have not yet integrated social and mobile into their decision-making process, and who are actually a larger percentage of their customer base—closer to their brand, making them more social in the process. Dunkin' Donuts ran traditional ads during Monday Night Football that used Twitter's new Vine video service. These videos would feature hot and iced coffee cups squaring off on a football field to rerun key plays from the Monday night NFL game. This campaign was then expanded to allow Dunkin' Donuts' social community to ask questions of the NFL announcers that would be answered on air. ESPN called the campaign "groundbreaking" and frequently referenced it.[2]

Dunkin' Donuts was using traditional media, billboards, and television commercials, combined with social media, to create a social connection to their brand, something it then expanded with the #DDRedCarpet campaign (where community members could ask questions of their favorite star during award season via the television shows *Extra* and *Entertainment Tonight*) and ultimately with the #MyDunkin campaign in late 2013, which featured real consumer-created content.[3] Dunkin Donuts had integrated social and mobile into its traditional enterprise processes of marketing, sales, and operations.

All of these efforts support Dunkin' Donuts' main value position: good, quality coffee for the average Joe, concisely expressed in the "America Runs on Dunkin'" slogan. These integrated efforts constantly reinforced their message across multiple mediums and reinforced for consumers the message that their experience with Dunkin' Donuts' will be great no matter where they are. These efforts create a connection that not only brings customers into stores more frequently; it also improves the actual overall value of the brand for both the franchisor and the company itself. This approach compensates for the weak brand loyalty that the franchise business model creates, one that would have been very expensive to overcome before social media. Since the launch of its social media strategy, Dunkin' Donuts has earned the number one ranking for customer loyalty in the coffee category by Brand Keys.[4] This is social media tightly integrated into corporate strategy.

For Dunkin' Donuts, social and mobile are not only extensions of marketing, but also extensions of branding, Product Development, Sales, Operations, and many of the other departments and processes that support the core of their enterprise.

Every organization can connect big, social, mobile to their enterprise to realize many different benefits—let's look at each of the seven benefits mentioned earlier.

IDENTIFYING AND GAINING CONSUMERS MORE COST-EFFECTIVELY

Big Social Mobile enterprises use digital initiatives to reduce the cost of customer acquisition. Traditional methods relied on mass advertising and the physical location of facilities and assets to reach consumers, and lacked the precision necessary to distinguish which consumers could most easily be converted into actual customers. That precision was left to sales people. When combined, this effort represented a significant percentage of a company's overall expense.

A presence on social media, on the other hand, costs even less to create than a professional website, while professional-looking and functioning mobile apps can be created by wizard-type functionality that never requires interaction with a real person. Posting content via any social media platform is free, aside from the salary of the posting employee. Given time, and even the most basic, segregated approach, any company can build an online, social community.

Big Social Mobile enterprises, though, can do a lot more than simply foster community growth. While integrated enterprises see even this fledgling effort as valuable, they also possess a larger vision for that community and see it as made up of consumers who could be sold to, current customers who could be upsold, influential people who can promote their brand, and people with whom they can solicit feedback to help their company improve and grow.

Integrated enterprises also mine their communities for information—derived from big data—on what will most successfully draw new people into this community, increase their engagement, and influence them to behave in ways that benefit their organization. Because of the continuous and seamless flow of information between consumers and all organizational functions, these companies can increase engagement in ways that go beyond the typical social media definition—they can help create meaningful relationships between consumers and Sales and Operations.

Big Social Mobile enterprises have a constant feedback loop that uses their social communities to test new approaches, survey responses, solicit specific feedback on improvement, and distribute this information throughout their organization, thereby improving their approach. This works to grow their community, launch effective marketing campaigns, successfully introduce new products and services, and improve their internal operations. Through digital initiatives, they can leverage their most passionate and supportive consumers to help them better understand and approach the market at a relatively low cost, especially when compared to the blunt-pencil approach of traditional mass media marketing and Sales.

The superior content an integrated approach provides also facilitates effective relationships with customers. Consumers want more than just the marketing content of a company reformatted and delivered via social media (what has become the norm)—they want more meaningful insight into how the product or service works, how it adds value to their life, and how they can get it for the lowest cost possible. They also expect the person with whom they interact with via social or mobile platforms to be more than a talking head—a key distinction between a segregated and an integrated approach. When organizations provide their social communities with value-based content created or delivered by the right people, communities grow, engagement deepens, propensity to purchase improves, and loyalty increases.

A segregated company never realizes these benefits. Their social media expert posts marketing content intended to convince consumers to buy. He or she might also post general industry information, holiday messages, and general company information. But once a consumer purchases a product, the marketing content has achieved its purchase and the content has lost its value. Put another way, of what value to the consumer is any ongoing connection to the company through social or mobile technology if its only intent is to sell them? Maintaining the social connection is not creating any additional value. If the customer has a problem, he or she is lucky if the social analyst within a segregated organization directs them to Customer Service or web content that could solve their problem—actions social consumers could easily take on their own. Contrast this with a social media feed that goes into deeper detail on new, creative uses for the product a consumer purchased. This is expert-created content that people typically don't have access to, and making it available gives consumers a reason to remain attached to the brand.

The benefit for Big Social Mobile enterprises is that they're measuring success not by the limited measures of followers, users, engagement, or data collected but rather by the more meaningful metrics of opportunities generated, consumers converted to customers revenue, expense reduction, or customer lifetime value. Valuable content creates these beneficial effects within the social community; meaningless content does not.

Consider, too, that customers are likely to stay with a company that delivers truly valuable content. When people need to replace or upgrade the product they purchased, they are unlikely to switch and forsake rich content unless there is a significant price difference. Valuable content is "sticky." It increases customer retention and customer lifetime value—it delivers hard returns.

Search engines have made this benefit even more essential. They have become more sophisticated in their measurements, assessing the value of the content being delivered, not just the amount. Today, search engines have evolved to a point where companies must be conscious of the content they deliver via the web; self-serving marketing content can actually hurt their ranking in search engines.

FACILITATING MICRO-MARKETING

By analyzing the big data associated with consumer behavior, companies can not only target consumers who are most likely to become customers, but also time their interactions exactly when each consumer is most likely to become a customer. By analyzing search keywords contained in big data, the photography and imaging consumer goods company mentioned in the previous chapter was able to tell when a consumer was planning a big vacation. Traditional enterprise data, including survey questions included during the product registration process that asked what prompted a customer's purchase, had long proven that a high percentage of customers upgraded their camera right before a big vacation (see Figure 2.1). By combining these two pieces of information—i.e., by integrating big data with enterprise information—the company was able to target these potential customers at exactly the right time, even while they were researching a competitor's product, sometimes stealing them away while they were standing beside a competitor's salesperson in a retail establishment.

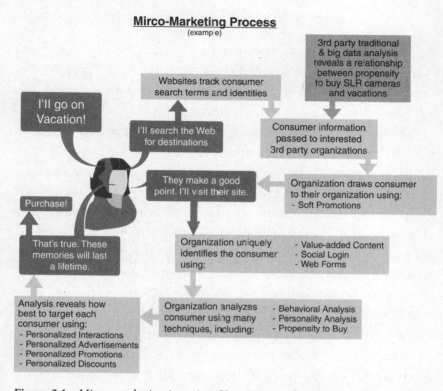

Figure 2.1 Micro-marketing in action. How integrated enterprises key off specific consumer behaviors and combine interactions across various mediums to uncover opportunities.

In a truly integrated enterprise, this marketing strategy can be automated by technology that actively looks for behaviors or patterns and responds with specific, highly personalized communications, information, or offers when that exact right moment arrives. For example, when a search engine flags vacation search terms, a sidebar advertisement for cameras can be prompted, followed up by email or banner ads that highlight the value of capturing memories that will last a lifetime over the next few days. This highly targeted marketing, or what I call *micro-marketing*, was never before possible; it was simply too expensive using traditional methods.

If social media, mobile technology, and big data are used in the proper manner—tightly integrated into each other and into the enterprise itself—information can be gathered and analyzed to yield greater perception into a consumer's wants and needs, improving the success of highly targeted and personalized messages.

UNCOVERING POTENTIAL NEW CUSTOMERS

Big Social Mobile enterprises can expose their products and services to groups of consumers who were previously unreachable. But this is only possible when companies integrate data generated from interactions with consumers into mainstream business functions and decision making.

Prior to the social media revolution, a company always led with its brand, via its name, logo, or tag line, or with its product, via the product name, its picture or logo, or its marketing slogan. This was necessary because mass marketing—television, radio, print, email, websites and even text—is based upon a *push* technique. Companies pushed their message out to as wide an audience as possible and hoped their name or product would stick in the minds of consumers and result in a purchase when the right moment came. Push marketing was necessary because it was difficult for companies to identify exactly when consumers wanted or needed their product—what is called *pull* marketing.

Pull techniques are more effective because when people have expressed a need for a product they are much more likely to buy; pull methods are more successful at converting consumers to customers. Social media and mobile technology are all based upon pull philosophy (although push techniques are often implemented via these platforms) because they are predominantly consumer technologies. Consumers use social or mobile to find what they are interested in, and if they "like" or follow a brand, it signified that they are interested in the company and what it has to offer.

Yet at some point organizations will reach a point of customer saturation—social and mobile techniques no longer pull in many consumers because they've all been pulled in by one company or another. When this occurs the only way to grow is to steal each individual customer from a competitor—typically using discounts. This is not an optimal growth strategy for many reasons, whether using traditional approaches or social media. Big Social Mobile enterprises, though, have another option.

An integrated approach makes it possible for a company to associate their brand with something that appeals to a group of consumers totally outside of their target market—what I call *associative marketing*. Associative marketing is based upon the premise that there can be value in this association itself, especially in fully saturated market segments, because data itself is valuable to Big Social Mobile enterprises; they gather, analyze and use the information contained in big data in creative ways to grow their customer base.

This is exactly what Proctor & Gamble did with their woman's deodorant brand Secret by associating it with an anti-bullying campaign called "Bullying Stinks." On the Bullying Stinks website that Proctor & Gamble supports, the Secret logo is visible, but the website's focus is clearly on what consumers are passionate about: the negative impact of bullying. Conventional logic holds that the Secret brand is earning goodwill among its consumer base, many of whom are woman, but that it's unlikely to spur a real increase in market share (because it is a fully saturated market) and therefore is not worth the cost. But by employing the associative marketing technique, the company is able to use this passionate connection to achieve two objectives.

First, the website captures the personal, demographic, and behavioral data of every member, many of whom are woman and some who are not current customers. Proctor & Gamble can then directly target these consumers using social and mobile techniques to incrementally grow sales in a way that is far cheaper than could be done traditionally and would not even be possible if they did not have a way to capture this information. At the same time the company is growing its community and gaining long-term insight into a much broader community than they could obtain through their own social initiative. The Bullying Stinks campaign is creating a corporate asset—information. And this information is then integrated into every function of the enterprise to drive growth and create product and operational improvements—it is not confined to social media experts.

Second, some of the members of the Bullying Stinks community will be men or young girls who do not yet purchase their own deodorant. Proctor & Gamble also mines data about these community members who can then be targeted, again using incrementally inexpensive social and mobile techniques that capitalize on the goodwill the brand has built through their anti-bullying campaign. When these individual consumers are in a situation where they can influence the purchase of woman's deodorant—a young girl going shopping on her own for the first time or a father stopping at the supermarket with his daughter or for his wife—the brand is at top of their mind. When the product arrives in the consumer's home, a discussion may ensue about why this particular product was chosen and not the typical household brand. In some cases, the conversation will focus upon the anti-bullying campaign, reinforcing the passionate connection between anti-bullying and the brand (see Figure 2.2).

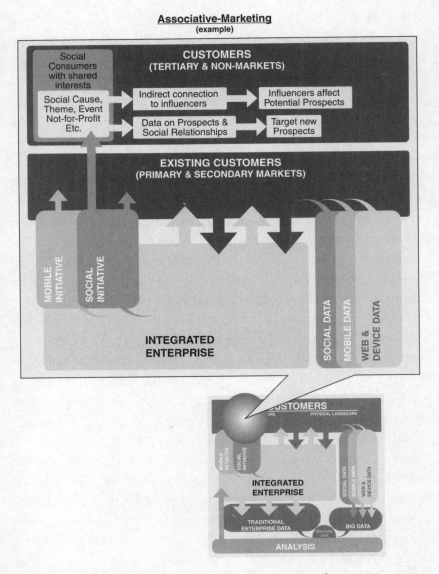

Figure 2.2 Associative marketing in action. How integrated enterprises uncover new market segments by associating their brand with social causes, themes, events, not-for-profit organizations, and other consumer interests.

To carry out this type of associative marketing campaign, corporate thinking must be wide-ranging and interconnected. To capture and leverage data that exist "outside of the box," social media experts, researchers, marketing and sales specialists, corporate leaders, and others must be included in the planning, data analysis, and outreach efforts. This is the only way that a bold associative marketing campaign makes its way from idea to implementation. Given that it defies the conventional wisdom, it requires the support of top executives. It demands that a diverse group of corporate specialists put their heads together to determine the right cause to associate with and the unorthodox audience to target. Many different corporate perspectives must come together to maximize its value to the organization.

If these requirements are fulfilled, companies can uncover new markets for their product using this new method.

IMPROVED CONSUMER TARGETING

The big data that social media and mobile technology generate is often praised for its ability to help companies understand consumer behavior, to see and play the long game better than ever before. This is often done by looking at the trends associated with different market segments and key demographic groupings that a company markets to—for example, of all the new functionality that could be added to a specific product, which will consumers actually pay more for? Big Social Mobile enterprises use the information generated from big data for this purpose within each area of their business, but also leverage this information in another, very different way.

On the journey to becoming Big Social Mobile, executives become increasingly aware that their approach allows them to go beyond just marketing to the right people; they can now reach the right people with the right message at exactly the right time. They understand that to group men buying via their web channel into groups based upon age, such as 25–34, is simply too generalized. They can gain better engagement, increase mindshare, and have a greater chance of influencing buying behavior when they create smaller sub-segments of their target market; they can take a more personalized and results-oriented approach with these smaller groups. This represents a tactical use of big data, and integrated enterprises are able to take advantage of it because of their high level of internal connectivity.

To use big data tactically, organizations must segment the market into increasingly smaller groups to make content sufficiently personable. They can then create smaller, tighter messaging that will have a greater impact upon the individual group members. For instance, a retailer can target a specific consumer in a specific aisle getting ready to make a decision about buying a television; they can dispatch a salesperson to meet this prospective buyer, increasing the likelihood of a purchase being made. Consider another example: an automotive dealership that uses a television campaign to not only advertise but also to create a social connection with consumers looking to purchase a new car, starting a dialogue with them, and thereby collecting their information and beginning to build a relationship with them. Or a camera company that targets consumers to upgrade from a smart phone to a consumer-grade SLR camera right before they go on vacation because big data has told them that at that exact moment they are more likely to be receptive.

None of these targeted benefits will be realized unless the gathered information is embedded into different functional areas and core process throughout the enterprise. There has to be an infrastructure that alerts a sales associate that a customer is in the final stages of making a decision about buying a television, automobile, or camera. This infrastructure must also provide sales personnel with insights into how to interact with, help educate, and counter the behaviors of highly social and mobile consumers. Marketing might get the consumer to the right isle, but Sales must interact with them to close the deal. This requires an integrated approach: Sales, Marketing, and Operations must work together based upon knowledge gained by analyzing big data. The process must be driven by a Marketing person and a Sales person who both understand and agree upon the options that the social consumer has available to them and the best tactic for communicating with that individual.

If that salesperson shows up at the point of purchase and does little more than ask if the shopper needs help, today's social consumer is likely to decline assistance; empowered consumers aren't likely to respond positively to a generalized offer of help. And, in many cases, social consumers know how to access competitive information better than an untrained salesperson. But if that salesperson is armed with knowledge derived from analysis and is advised by the right people within the organization, then the balance of power shifts; the salesperson can utilize a mobile device to help the potential customer do the research necessary to decide whether to buy. Perhaps even more important, this also requires that the salesperson has even more information on how to make the offer more appealing than that of a competitor. Doing this requires an integrated approach: a sales department that has worked with their social media staff to understand a consumer's social options, incorporated into training delivered by the human resource department so that the sales person is prepared; a sales department that has already worked with big data analysts to understand and put in place a process that gives their sales people, or their sales managers, the right pricing or incentive options that counter competitive behavior; a sales department that has worked with their financial analysts to understand the behaviors that impact total customer lifetime value so that they are not giving away more profit than necessary.

Creating the tight integration that allows for these behaviors within an enterprise might seem challenging; it is. But it's a challenge that any Big Social Mobile organization can meet—and must meet to remain competitive.

INCREASING CREDIBILITY USING THIRD PARTIES

The value of third-party endorsements is undisputed; marketers grasp that people are much more likely to become a customer based on an impartial recommendation of a product or service versus an impersonal (though much more expensive) marketing campaign featuring advertising, sales promotion, and so on. This is why Amazon and so many other companies feature reviews from unknown consumers. These reviews aid would-be buyers in the narrowing-down process, giving them the extra confidence they often need to make the purchase on the spot. In this same way, even companies with highly segregated approaches still enjoy the benefits of leveraging third parties to help them sell. An integrated approach, though, capitalizes on a much larger number and greater diversity of influential third parties. Just as important, this approach creates credibility through those individuals I refer to as *Social Influencers*.

Social Influencers are those people who have access to a large number of consumers within the company's target audience over which they exert influence to affect their decision making or opinion. Big Social Mobile enterprises understand who these influencers are within their social communities and actively build relationships with them. Further, they grasp that these influencers' power is based upon their perceived impartiality. If they were hired by a company, overnight their influence would evaporate. Integrated enterprises, therefore, do not co-opt these influencers in any way or create schemes that hide the fact that influencers are being rewarded. Instead, Big Social Mobile enterprises expose these influencers to, and help them understand, the value of what a company has to offer through blogs, posts on social platforms, video demonstrations, and even personal interactions. This is what Amazon's Vine service seeks to do. It provides their most respected reviewers with access to new products so that they can write the first online reviews. This provides an impartial third-party perspective that helps consumers understand these products and their value, earning Amazon goodwill as a trusted source of impartial information.

Part of the integrated approach relies upon social and mobile being a clear reflection of the company's culture and core value proposition; they cannot fake value. They don't try to make the organization seem "hipper" or alter its strategy or mission to make a better impression on influencers. Instead, they take their core value proposition and reinforce it—clearly communicating what defines the company, consistently and powerfully.

In this way, organizations develop honest, open, two-way relationships with Social Influencers. Companies bend over backward to share information with these influencers, to answer their questions, to put them in touch with key people throughout the organization—everyone from social media experts to R&D to the CEO. In turn, these influencers are responsive and willing to provide the organization with a tremendously valuable third-party endorsement. This endorsement may also expose some of the company's weaknesses, but that is part of what makes the Social Influencer trusted—and influential.

The way Big Social Mobile enterprises build relationships with Social Influencers is reflective of how they utilize their entire social community. They actively solicit members that will help them discover the next great product or service innovation, to create more effective or efficient processes and generate better content, to design a superior mobile application, and to expose them to new markets.

IMPROVING CUSTOMER SATISFACTION

Integrating big, social, and mobile initiatives with one another creates synergies. Mobile efforts become more social; the social techniques and messages become embedded into mobile technology; the voice of the enterprise becomes one over time. Big data then begins providing insight into how successfully these now-identical initiatives are influencing and affecting consumers.

However, if this is the extent of the integration—if these initiatives are not integrated into the enterprise itself—then the enterprise will begin to duplicate functions. As customers begin using social media for product inquiries, the company's social analysts will begin to function as sales people or engineers; as customers begin to use social media to have their problems addressed, these same analysts or digital marketers will begin to function as customer service representatives. Not only is it wasteful to have duplicate functions, but social media professionals should not be handling functions outside of their area of expertise. In a truly integrated enterprise, customer questions and feedback are directed to the employees that specialize in helping them, not to those who have little knowledge of how to interact with customers, answer product-oriented questions, or offer insight into products and services. In fact, when you find an organization that has a "social customer service" department, it's a clear sign of a segregated mind-set—social media analysts shouldn't be functioning as customer service agents; they have no training, expertise, or experience.

When big, social, and mobile are embedded into the enterprise, customer service inquiries received through any channel are directed toward the customer service department; sales inquiries or opportunities spotted by any employee using traditional, social, or mobile channels are directed toward Sales. The primary function of each department remains the same, with those in charge of social and mobile directing traffic, or controlling processes that direct traffic, as necessary. Consumers use phones, email, direct chat, social feeds, and mobile apps to access whomever they need within the enterprise, in the way that is easiest for the consumer. Behind the scenes, the company is working hard to ensure that the processes supporting these separate mediums of communication are consistent. But of even more value is the positive experience that consumers are having in addition to the value they are realizing from the company's product or service itself. And they are sharing this positive experience throughout their entire social network.

Big Social Mobile enterprises also satisfy consumers by providing them with direct access to information whenever possible, without the need to interact with company employees. For instance, their mobile apps show what products the company offers, in which stores it is available, and also the inventory level within each store, so that consumers don't waste a trip to a retail establishment, becoming frustrated in the process.

Consumers can order online, through a mobile app or via phone, and then have the product drop shipped or waiting for pickup at any store. And when customers arrive to pick up their order, they don't have to wait in a checkout line. They have a separate pickup area, getting them in and out of the store as quickly as possible.

To provide this benefit of increased consumer satisfaction, organizational leaders must embrace the new logic of social consumers. In the past, organizations would have considered it unthinkable to allow a customer to enter and exit a physical location without maximizing the customer's in-store time. There's a reason escalators put you deeper into a store before allowing you to exit or why the most common consumables are placed at the farthest end of an aisle. This is traditional manipulation of a consumer.

While integrated organizations certainly hope to sell to consumers while they're onsite, they also recognize and prioritize the big, social, and mobile gestalt. They would rather sacrifice an in-store opportunity to sell in exchange for giving consumers the opportunity to interact with and obtain valuable information from the company in the way that the new social consumer prefers. These companies believe that the more positive the experience, the more loyal consumers are to the brand. Some Big Social Mobile enterprises are even allowing consumers to shop throughout the store, scan items, place them in their shopping cart and exit the store without the need to interact with any store employee. Billing and delivery of an electronic receipt is done automatically, storing their information to make it easier for shoppers next time they return to the store. They don't have to remember easily forgotten shopping details the next they return to the store—the type of printer a consumer needs ink for, or the brand, favorite flavor, or proper size for each family member. Integrated enterprises open their systems to consumers and facilitate their access to information and online assistance.

It is important to remember that these companies are doing all of this because it not only improves consumers' satisfaction but also because it generates more revenue per customer, per shopping experience, and per each customer's lifetime, while also improving customer loyalty, the brand's reputation, and the efficiency and effectiveness of internal processes.

SHAPING CONSUMER BEHAVIOR

Smart companies have always understood that each step in their marketing and sales process is designed to do one thing: motivate the customer to purchase their product or service. Every advertisement, brochure, marketing pitch, or sales presentation is designed to move the customer toward that moment of conversion. With the arrival of social media and mobile technology, though, many companies feel as if they have lost control over the consumer's decision-making process. Customers can now stand in their store and look at impartial third-party reviews, non-company educational videos, or even competitive pricing. This sense of lost control is due to many factors—social and mobile being consumer-controlled technologies, the shift toward pull marketing, and reduced barriers to entry for smaller competitors.

Big Social Mobile enterprises accept this loss of control and adapt to these new dynamics, while segregated organizations avoid dealing with these changes by considering them only social and mobile problems. There is a historical parallel between how companies are handling this loss of power and how quickly some companies adapted to the Internet, while other struggled. The Internet was the first major technology to erode corporate power because it distributed information so effectively. Companies quick to adapt responded by becoming "customer-centric."

Customer-centric organizations view themselves through the eyes of the consumer. These companies analyze every personal interaction, process, and technology that a consumer encounters on their journey to becoming a satisfied customer to ensure that each contributes to the best overall experience possible. They try to create the best and most consistent overall experience. For example, within power utilities—an industry notorious for its monopoly mindset because consumers lack options—a traditional enterprise puts emphasis on power generation and power delivery, investing in engineers and technology that support them; customers are treated indifferently and customer service is often understaffed, relying on old technology.

Some power utilities, especially municipal utilities that are owned by their customers, have chosen to become customer-centric. These progressively minded utilities understand that consumer opinion is not shaped by power generation and delivery and the army of expensive engineers with whom customers never interact, but rather by the lowest-paid employees in the often-understaffed customer call center.

Management in a customer-centric power utility understands that there is both a hard and soft cost associated with mass-scale customer dissatisfaction, just as there are tangible benefits to satisfied customers—for example, surveys show that satisfied customers will pay slightly higher prices. Therefore, they ensure that a department such as customer service receives equal priority in the distribution of resources. Power generation and delivery are still important, and inherently more expensive, but their importance is relative to their impact on the overall customer experience.

Customer-centric companies inherently make the transition to becoming Big Social Mobile more smoothly because they already understand that the consumer's perspective has a tangible impact on value. Big Social Mobile enterprises simply take this concept to the next level. Integration provides them with the mentality and the means to not only understand the customer experience better than ever before but to measure and use it to their best advantage.

Integrated enterprises collect and use information about process efficiency and combine it with social and behavioral information contained within big data. Big data is so big not because it helps companies understand trends with broad brushes (what companies have traditionally used it for), but because it is so precise in detailing the experience for each individual consumer. Integrated enterprises possess insight into the intricate social community each person is part of; to a large extent they know each time customers interact with their brand; they can track their physical locations during these interactions and the technology they are using. They also know quite a bit about consumers on a personal level. They know who they are friends with, what social influencers they respect, what their personal interests are and even events that are going on in their life.

All of this information restores the balance of power between corporations and consumers, and integrated enterprises are in the best position to use this regained power. They create systems that ensure that this information flows strategically to just the right employee within the organization at just the right time; and that these employees have the mandate to use this information to achieve larger organizational goals.

The photography and imaging consumer goods company previously mentioned was one of the first to apply this technique to shape interactions with consumers. Their customer service agents would see a series of icons appear next to the customer's account information when they called. These icons drew on social and mobile data to provide the agent with insight into what the customer's current sentiment might be, and how influential they were deemed within the social community. Sometimes the agent would know exactly why they were calling before they even started the conversation. Agents were also alerted about past interactions, required information or potential items that might have led to the call. When combined, this allowed the agent to understand not only who the customer was and what their current mind-set was likely to be at that exact moment, but also the overall estimated "worth" of that customer to the company. This shaped the entire interaction, everything from what additional products or services might appeal to them, to what additional discounts and promotions it made sense to offer them, if necessary.

This type of highly personalized interaction appeals to today's social consumer. They expect to have a relationship with the brands they purchase from. This is allowing companies to begin to shift the power back in their favor, toward those things that most benefit the company, ensuring that consumers understand not only their core value proposition but also the philosophy behind it- why they do what they do, why they do it the way they do, and how consumers should be benefiting from it. All of these things add up to reinforce the value of the consumer maintaining an ongoing relationship with the company.

* * *

The road to realizing all of these benefits begins with an acceptance that big data, social media, and mobile technology are all part of one bigger movement that has changed some of the basic market dynamics companies have grown used to. These benefits are not as unreachable as most executives might think. Most organizations already have these building blocks in place. They possess social media programs, mobile applications, and nearly all of the technology that manages data and transforms it into information. Therefore, it becomes more about using these assets in a new way and less about creating something new—more about properly aligning the organization rather than reinventing it.

Achieving this has its challenges, which we'll explore next.

Chapter 3

OBSTACLES TO INTEGRATION

EXECUTIVES HAVE BEEN BOMBARDED BY ONE digital initiative after another during the last decade—social media, mobile technology, and big data. In response to this rapid change, creating separate initiatives seems to make sense. It's a logical reaction to hire and allow subject-matter experts to build the infrastructure, programs, and approaches that will work to address these new demands. This is, after all, how organizations have dealt with similar initiatives in the past. Six Sigma, Lean, Kaizen, Just-In-Time inventory, open sourcing, outsourcing, reverse innovation, and risk management all have been handled by creating new initiatives. Some added lasting value while others didn't. But when these trends faded, companies went back to business as usual.

Many companies have handled these new digital initiatives as they have handled others in the past—they've launched initiatives but haven't seen a need to address their larger implications, believing that given enough time, these too will fade. But these are not hype-driven management trends. They are consumer trends, reflecting fundamental changes in consumer behavior. And consumers will not suddenly give up the power social media has given them; they will not become less mobile. Therefore, nearly all of the significant obstacles organizations face while becoming Big Social Mobile stem from this conflict between how companies have traditionally dealt with the changes initiatives have placed upon them and how these traditional approaches conflict with the demands of today's social consumer.

THE EIGHT-YEAR RULE

Never before have companies been at such odds with consumers. The traditional approach of creating segmented initiatives to deal with new market-driven demands fails to address new consumer concerns and needs effectively, although to organizations they seem to be doing the job—creating large communities of followers that are actively engaged with their organization. But big data, social media, and mobile technology actually require a different response than the norm. If we continue to treat these changes as we did those in the past, we will unknowingly create obstacles to integration.

Consider the first major digital development that prompted a significant change in consumer behavior was handled: the Internet. By now, most business readers are familiar with its simple beginnings as a way for Department of Defense scientists to share information and its stagnant growth until the 1990s, where it reached a peak size of approximately 4,000 institutions. In 1995 it was decommissioned from government control and quickly grew to over 16 million users; by the year 2000, there were over 300 million users; a billion by 2005.[1] By 2015 Internet usage will exceed 3 billion individual users—an 18,650 percent growth rate in personal use in 20 years.

This is consumer-driven change; it reflects the most rapid adoption rate of any technology in history. Even smart phones, tablets, laptops, and computers have not come close. Companies had no other option but to respond, and most of them initially responded with a segregated approach.

Symbolics.com, a Massachusetts-based computer manufacturer, was the first to respond in 1985, registering the first domain and kicking off the .com and .net structure we know today.[2] But despite its early adoption of this new consumer-based technology, Symbolics was actually slow to adapt to the changes it represented. Former Symbolics employee Dan Weinreb explains: "The world changed out from under us very quickly...We at Symbolics were slow to acknowledge this. We believed our own 'dogma' even as it became less true. It was embedded in our corporate culture. If you disputed it, your co-workers felt that you 'just didn't get it' and weren't a member of the clan, so to speak. This stifled objective analysis. (This is a very easy problem to fall into—don't let it happen to you!)."[3]

Within ten years Symbolics was bankrupt.

From that first .com the Internet has grown to over 275 million active domains—entities or individuals operating as entities—conducting commerce or information sharing via the Internet through a fixed web address.[4] But this number is misleading.

The digital world operates the same as any land-based community. A domain is essentially the same as a physical location in the real world. It is connected to other sites via links that form the streets upon which consumers travel to locate the goods, services, and information they desire. Within these small digital communities consumers encounter others who share common attitudes, interests, and goals that are mutually re-enforcing—the very definition of a community. But a community is not stable. People come and go; companies succeed and fail.

Across the entire digital landscape 15 percent of Internet locations are empty lots owned by someone but sitting idle and empty. Another 21 percent are the equivalent of under construction or coming soon, or are so simple they offer little benefit to consumers. Only 64 percent of the Internet locations, or domains, consist of multipage sites that will actually help make consumers' lives better, or at least more interesting.[5] That means that only 180 million of the 275 million domains are active in the true sense of the word. And just like in the real world, some of these are in the process of going out of business—50 percent of small businesses in the real world fail within the first five years of their existence.[6]

According to WhoIs, over 75,000 Internet domains are abandoned each day—approximately 1 million per year. Larger companies, such as the bankrupt Symbolics, possess enough capital power, assets, or intellectual property to sell their business. As legal ownership of these companies changes hand in the real world their digital assets, including the digital land they own, changes hands. This occurs over 270,000 times per day or 3.2 million times per year, with most of these domains eventually merging into the purchasing entity's domain.

It is this behavior that makes the 275 million entities or individuals operating via the Internet misleading. Even the adjusted number of 180 million entities actively operating via the Internet is misleading when compared to the additional 4.2 million entities that come and go from the Internet each year.

But this still doesn't tell the entire story. All of these numbers actually need to be calculated cumulatively *back to the very beginning of the Internet itself.* In approximately three decades, the Internet has accumulated only 180 million or so entities currently using it to conduct business or share information, whereas that same number fails every 8.5 years, at the current rate.

Again, here in the real world 50 percent of new companies fail within five years. For larger corporations the number is much lower: only 10 percent fail each year. In the digital world the equivalent of the entire community conducting business dies every 8.5 years.

What does this mean?

Symbolics actually beat the odds. The vast majority of companies that attempt to compete in the digital world, where more and more consumers are spending their time, fail—and fail quickly. This is because the segregated approach they adopt fails to accommodate the larger consumer-driven changes that digital initiatives such as the Internet, and social media and mobile technology, create. Organizations must fully commit to meeting the changing demands of today's highly social, highly mobile, information-driven consumer or they will not remain viable for long—as we will see throughout this book in several examples of well-known companies that have fallen prey to the Eight-Year Rule.

THE CORPORATE-CONSUMER RELATIONSHIP

The Internet prompted a change in consumer behavior that has created an overarching obstacle for organizations. After the Internet became established, companies were able to deal with this obstacle by making sure each department's core functions were mirrored on their websites. The ability to find information, request Marketing or Sales literature, place an order, or contact Customer Service were consumer expectations at that time. But as social media and mobile technology took hold, the consumer became more empowered, demanding a fundamental shift in the corporate mind-set—a shift from segregated to integrated thinking. Unfortunately, this shift has not occurred in most organizations—or has been erratic and piecemeal—and has caused companies to struggle with how they relate to the growing power consumers now possess. Consumers will no longer respond to the attitudes, approaches, and processes that companies relied upon in the past—they will no longer become customers if corporations will not meet them on their own terms.

To overcome the obstacle that an empowered consumer presents, organizations must create a seamless, cross-channel experience (sometimes called an omni-channel) for all the stakeholders who cross their digital path. Consumers not only expect to receive the same product or services at the same price via multiple modes of distribution—retail store, web, phone, third-party sales, social, or mobile—they also expect the same level of service, responsiveness and understanding from each employee they interact with, both personally and digitally, through each of these channels. Today, consumers have little tolerance for entering personal information into a phone-bot only to be asked for the same information again by the Customer Service Agent. Social consumers expect every employee to understand their needs and respond with information that is specific to them. However, most organizations do not have the processes set up or the information available to provide this seamless response to customer inquires coming in via social or mobile technology and their multiple traditional channels.

Powerful consumers are particularly vexing to organizations because these consumers can now influence the brand reputation of even the largest and most powerful corporations. In 2009 United Airlines damaged guitarist David Carroll's custom guitar and refused to resolve the situation. As of the writing of this book, the video he created about the incident has received over 13 million views on YouTube alone, millions of additional views on other social platforms and news outlets, and has become a standard business school case study. United Airlines finally did offer to resolve the situation, but not until significant damage had been done to the brand.

This incident marks one of the first displays of consumer power. Digital initiatives, beginning with the Internet, have created a fundamental shift in the relationship between companies or controlling entities and the consumer, what I call the *corporate-consumer relationship*. When companies fail to acknowledge that power has shifted from the corporation to the consumer, they lack the motivation to integrate big, social, and mobile into their enterprise. They persist in believing that a lone consumer—even one as motivated as David Carroll—can't really cause much harm to their organization.

To overcome this counterproductive thinking, organizations must focus on the proper use of information. By embedding information into all business processes—information about consumers and the other options from competitors that they now have easy access to—organizations can provide a seamless experience across channels (what is often called an "omni-channel" experience) and spot and resolve potential individual problems before they become national news stories or cause other headaches. Both corporations and consumers now have greater access to information; consumers are committed to using it. To be successful, organizations must be equally savvy and committed.

Most of the information consumers are using to gain the upper hand has always been available, but was never easily accessible. The Internet made this possible; social media made it mainstream; mobile technology, as the constant companion to the consumer, has made it a problem for corporations that simply cannot be ignored.

It is understandable, however, why organizations do ignore or minimize the obstacles created by empowered consumers. History exerts a powerful influence on the corporate mind-set, and consumers have not had or asserted dominance over corporations in over 500 years.

Over 500 years ago, before the arrival of the wage-labor economic model, individuals traded goods based upon need and relative value, what would be a direct *consumer-consumer relationship* or a non-technical form of today's eBay, where a price is reached based upon a supply-demand or perhaps more accurately a need-value tradeoff between individuals. Individual merchants gained a reputation in their community (probably just their town or nearby towns)

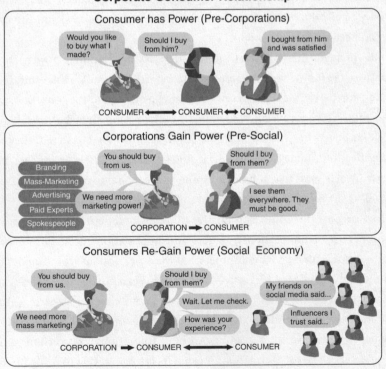

Figure 3.1   The shifting balance of power in the corporate-consumer relationship.

based upon the quality of their goods, and this reputation preceded them wherever they went. Although transactions were conducted between individuals, the community itself was acting as an "internal control," determining relative worth based upon three factors—availability, relative value, and quality. This information made individuals powerful; they had economic power and could bargain more effectively.

Over time, individuals stopped trading consumer to consumer and began trading their time to an employer for money, and this money was then traded for what they needed. The consumer-consumer relationship was replaced by the corporate-consumer relationship. This is the wage-labor system in use today—where a person's labor is literally exchanged for a wage. And within this new system, the majority of people had only one resource to trade: their time. Individuals no longer had power, other than through the amount of capital at their disposal; corporations (or companies or entities) had gained substantially more power, especially economic power [See Figure 3.1].

Corporations did not gain this power because they wielded greater economic wealth, as is commonly thought. They gained power because one technology after another allowed them to operate across increasingly larger areas, until by the turn of the twenty-first century, the Internet had fully globalized commerce. This growth of operating area removed the consumer's internal control. Word of mouth could no longer travel as far as corporations could reach. Mass media advertising influenced consumer opinion more than any localized reputations and corporations constructed sophisticated marketing and sales processes designed to turn consumers into customers as rapidly as possible, at the highest level of profitability possible. To make matters worse, because corporations had near complete control, they weren't creating processes centered upon helping consumers understand value; their processes were designed entirely around this conversion process. From the layout of escalators through department stores, to the ethnicity and demographic characteristics of fashion models and background elements in commercials, to product names, logos, and color schemes. The goal was to manipulate consumer opinion and behavior in a way that yielded the highest conversion rate and the highest profitability. Missing was any broad consumer check-and-balance.

From a consumer's perspective this may seem unethical, but from a corporate perspective this is the purpose that they were created for and the promise they make to their consumer-shareholders: maximizing profit.

The *quality* of service, for the average company, became the minimum acceptable. Some companies used high quality of service or customer care as a differentiator—Nordstrom, Southwest Airlines, or Dell, for example—but the average company placed less emphasis on customer service or quality (even though they rarely admit it), than they did on customer generation. The Internet did something more than just globalize competition. It would take years for consumers to realize it—actually until Facebook became the dominant social media platform in 2004—but the Internet allowed consumers to gain back power in this corporate-consumer relationship, and perhaps more importantly it changed their expectations. Consumers came to expect quality; not only quality goods and services, but also quality interactions.

Social media also gave consumers back their "internal control." They could now communicate across the entire operating area of even a fully globalized corporation, totally outside of systems controlled by the corporation, to discuss the relative worth of goods and services, their quality, and more importantly other options that consumers had. This new ability to communicate and share information has put consumers back in control.

Thus, the digital revolution has undone the 500 years of history upon which most of today's organizational structures, processes, and technologies are based. It's one thing to tell organizations that they should overcome the obstacle the empowered consumer presents; it's something else to do it, given 500 years of dealing with a disempowered consumer.

Fortunately, increased profitability is a powerful incentive to change, as our earlier examples of Starbucks and Dunkin' Donuts illustrated. So are continuously declining margins in the face of stiff competition. Today's leaders need to wrap their heads around the fact that consumers now have the upper hand and aren't going to relinquish it, and once they do that, they will find it easier to embrace an integrated approach.

THE MISUSE OF INFORMATION

Segregated organizations don't always understand the real value of information in the age of big data, and these misunderstandings prevent them from realizing the value contained within this data. They labor under preconceived and outmoded notions of what information is and how it is used. They fail to integrate it into business processes and strategy in a way that reflects performance across both the physical and digital landscapes. Three major misconceptions reinforce this segregated thinking, and stand in the way of organizations becoming Big Social Mobile.

MISCONCEPTION #1: IF WE COLLECT IT, VALUE WILL COME

Big data specialists within organizations are like fishermen dragging huge nets across the sea floor. They sweep up everything from fish to seaweed to old discarded shoes, but unfortunately they don't know what may be valuable, and what will be worthless, until they've already done the work of getting it into the boat. Because of the sheer quantity of social and mobile interactions being monitored, organizations quickly find themselves accumulating huge amounts of data about consumers and accumulating the high costs that go along with collecting, storing, and analyzing it. They can't determine its value until it has been collected and stored. And even then, these specialists cannot themselves determine the value of this data, and therefore the accumulation of data itself becomes the goal.

The term "big data" reinforces this thinking, encouraging management to think of the data and the technology required to support it and not the information that can be derived from it. Functional or departmental managers, who are concerned with information such as how many orders did we receive, by what channel, or how many calls did Customer Service receive versus how many were resolved, or even more complicated but traditional metrics such as margin per order, product, or customer, quickly dismiss the information contained within big data. They need information to answer business questions, not more—bigger—data.

As a result, big data is often considered important to only those specialists who deal with big data itself, or the social media or mobile initiatives that generate it. Statistics about followership, engagement, and adoption don't mean much to anyone outside of the social media and mobile technology groups and therefore it is never connected to the organization at large. Since mainstream managers have dismissed it, and these specialists don't know what to do with it, big data and the information contained within it remains segregated along with these initiatives.

The underlying cause of this segmentation is the lack of ability to translate this data into information that answers traditional business questions. And unlike traditional enterprise information, the bridge between this big-data-related information and traditional enterprise information has not yet been built. It remains unintegrated and underutilized.

MISCONCEPTION #2: THE COMPANY CAN DEMAND INFORMATION

Social media and mobile technology are unlike anything else that enterprises have encountered; they both represent user-owned technology. Users decide whether they will participate with companies via it, decide how they want to participate, and decide when not to participate. Organizations cannot control this. They must adapt their processes and design principles to accommodate user wants and needs, while at the same time ensuring that they add value to the consumer's experience and lives. The needs of the organization must come second to the wants of the user.

Consider the product registration process, or the "For More Information" web form. The primary desire of a company is to identify the person they are interacting with so that they can effectively target and make them a customer or upsell them. Traditionally, companies did this via a long and complicated process that included requests for extensive personal information. Consumers complied with these requests because they feared not being supported if they had problems. On a mobile app this same function is completed via the registration process. And the number one reason that consumers delete apps after they download them is a complicated or time-consuming registration process. Unlike their traditional counterpart, the social consumer will not tolerate cumbersome processes that are obvious in their intent to benefit the company; they will find another organization that better understands their desires. Users eventually delete 90 percent of all mobile apps they download, and with over 100 million active apps in the Apple marketplace alone, and over 1,000 new apps being added to it per day, they have plenty of other options.[7]

If organizations persist in the misconception that they can demand information from consumers, they will never obtain the information that truly integrated organizations require. They must create value in the interaction itself, and valuable information will follow.

MISCONCEPTION #3: ALL DATA ARE CREATED EQUAL

Traditional enterprise data and social and mobile big data are inherently different. Bringing the two together requires a change in both mind-set and technique. Traditional data and the information they create are exact and specific. There is only one version of an invoice or sales order, ordered by only one customer. A customer might be an organization that has multiple contact points within it, but the relationship is still relatively easily understood and quantified.

Big data, on the other hand, is inherently messy and incomplete. With big data it is often possible to tell that something happened—a person made a purchase, or contacted customer service, or requested more information—and it is possible to know many additional details about where that person was, what they were doing at the same time and potentially even what was nearby influencing them—all without knowing who the exact person is. Individuals can have separate or multiple profiles on different social or mobile platforms or choose not to reveal who they truly are altogether.

In addition, big data can never fully explain *why* something happened. There is no true causality between the actions that can be observed and the result. Therefore, the common, and limiting, organizational view of information within big data is that it is directional, providing broad insight, but it cannot be used for the specific purpose of improving bottom-line business results.

One leading big-box retailer proved this wrong. They found that they could determine when a shopper had entered into a significant relationship (before they officially changed their relationship status on social media) based upon the social information and behavioral patterns contained in big data related to that shopper. This customer's big data was integrated into the traditional enterprise data the company already had on that customer, to identify how this new relationship influenced the shopping pattern. Their analysis was so good that they could often determine which two shoppers had become a couple. They would then *micro-market* to each of the two customers using their partner's social data (such as what brands they liked) to suggest gifts. While they typically had to rely upon discounts to prompt an additional purchase from consumers, this retailer found that among these couples if they suggested the right product at a critical moment (such as an anniversary or after predetermined interval of time had passed) they could often solicit a purchase without offering any discount— and often increase the value of gifts as the relationship progressed and became more serious.

This usage of big data and its integration into traditional enterprise data overcomes the misconception that big data related information is solely directional, showing how Big Social Mobile enterprises collect, store, analyze, distribute and use this data differently than organizations that follow a segregated approach. They understand how to translate big data into actionable business information.

Thinking of information pulled from big data in this context is itself a foreign concept for many executives. Value is easily placed on information about customer orders, inventory fulfilment, and financial transactions because they are necessary to process customer orders effectively; they are necessary for the creation of profit. Some executives, especially within Sales groups, can see value in the detailed information stored within Customer Relationship Management software applications because it allows them to manage interactions with their customers and prospects and the opportunities that might generate new business. Some managers can see the value of a large social community that can be marketed to or a large number of users that interact with the enterprise through the more efficient functionality of a mobile application. But they often fail to grasp that the minor data points that accompany each social and mobile action or interaction—location, direction, speed, previous search terms, other applications installed or open, duration of usage, operating system specification, or even weather data—may have a significant impact upon the future success of their organization.

*   *   *

The retailer in the example mentioned above was able to use data in this new, creative, integrated fashion not only because it actively brought together big data and traditional enterprise data to create meaningful information, but also because it overcame the three information misconceptions I've described. It used information to tie the behavior of an unknown person—a random consumer in big data—to things that it did know, such as loyalty card numbers, cell phone numbers, and email addresses. In this way, it was able to identify specific people that customized marketing would appeal to based upon the patterns found in big data. This is micro-marketing in action. And micro-marketing has an advantage that traditional marketing does not. Once the idea and the linkages in data are determined, the technology will then do the work for the enterprise. The cost to penetrate the market incrementally is nearly zero dollars per transaction. There is true value in information; Big Social Mobile enterprises understand this and make the effort to overcome the obstacles that stand in the way of realizing this value.

LOSING SIGHT OF TRUE VALUE

As organizations work to adapt to the changes that digital initiatives have had on their organization, they often lose sight of their core value proposition or what consumers most value about them. The increased complexity that these digital initiatives create often distracts the organization from those things that made it successful in the first place, and from the objectives that generate tangible business results. This is an obstacle to the achievement of an integrated enterprise, and causes companies to fail in the digital world—as reflected in the Eight-Year Rule.

New social platforms, new mobile technology, additional communications mediums, and new Marketing and Sales channels all demand new processes and approaches to old things. Leaders, though, often become confused in this unfamiliar and rapidly changing environment. Some feel overwhelmed and become entrenched, believing they cannot burden their organization with entirely new approaches, technology, and consumer and competitive behavior that they don't fully comprehend. As a result, they refuse to change at all. They either come up with one excuse after another about why it is not yet the right time to launch any meaningful digital initiatives or they launch small, separate digital initiatives that have little tangible impact upon how the organization operates.

Others executives go to the opposite extreme, seeking to revolutionize themselves and their industry. They spend exorbitant amounts of money pursuing social and mobile strategies, hire additional staff, and fund the development of a variety of mobile apps. They try one approach after another, using the latest techniques only to find that in the end they may have grown large social communities, launched cool applications, and collected enormous amounts of data, but have found few tangible benefits.

Both of these reactions fail to produce the desired results because they disconnect the company's value proposition—what made that company valuable and unique—from the consumer. In the former instance, organizations can no longer communicate their value proposition effectively to a changed consumer, while in the later instance, they are so focused upon change that what the consumer values about the company is diminished or gone, swept away by change. In both situations, because they have either refused to change and see their company failing or they have tried multiple new techniques and not seen results, executives believe that they need to revolutionize the entire organization in order to compete effectively—they believe that only wholesale change will be effective.

I am all for revolutionary thinking if a revolution is called for, but for most organizations such thinking ends up hurting more than helping. In many cases, when organizations attempt to revolutionize, a belief persists that the accomplishments of the past must be set aside or that only sudden and marked change will achieve the necessary result. It forces the organization to lose touch with what made it unique in the first place—what customers have historically valued, such as their reputation for high quality, for responsible leadership, for affordability, or other differentiators. These are the value propositions upon which entire enterprises are built upon. They must be communicated to consumers on a constant and consistent basis.

Revolutionary thinking has caused problems for many organizations, most notably among them: Yahoo!. Yahoo! was created to revolutionize the Internet. At a time when most other websites used automated "spiders" programs to crawl the web, capturing, storing, and organizing the ever-growing list of websites and their content, the founders of Yahoo! believed that they had found an entirely new way to organize the contents of the dynamically growing World Wide Web. They were right; in only two years they created the first widely used Internet portal. Yahoo! went public for $85.8 million, $33 per share, and in 2000 it peaked at $500.13 per share.

The Yahoo! portal collected and categorized information on topics relevant to the user, anything from websites to weather to traffic patterns. But the World Wide Web was growing too fast, and the expert staff that they relied upon to evaluate each website couldn't be scaled effectively. They had to augment their personalized ranking with a simple search engine that allowed users to easily find other nonranked information they wanted. They outsourced this simple search functionality to an increasingly popular, spider-based search engine called Google. Google was becoming so popular that Yahoo! Internet Life even named it the "Best Search Engine on the Internet."

"We're extremely proud that Yahoo! has selected Google to complement its existing directory and navigational guide," added Sergey Brin, Google cofounder and president. "This is a significant milestone for Google and a strong validation of our business strategy."[8]

Less than a year later the Internet bubble burst. Yahoo! stock dropped to an all-time low of $8.02 per share, and after much criticism for not having created a search engine of its own, Yahoo! acquired two spider-based search engine companies and dropped their partnership with Google. This move marked a significant change in the company's focus. They would give up their personalized approach to user portals and become a spider-based search engine that used proprietary algorithms just like their competitors.

As a result, Yahoo! all but collapsed—in just over eight years. Google rapidly became the company and term synonymous with the Internet.

It may seem that Yahoo! failed because they gave up what made them unique: a portal of information that would provide users with everything they needed to enrich their daily lives. What the founders didn't realize, though, was that its users valued the Yahoo! site's ability to instantly search for information on any topic, not just topics that were relevant to their daily lives. Yahoo! had created the first widely-adopted Internet search engine inside of the portal they placed so much value upon. Their customers loved the search engine, not the portal.

Yahoo! didn't fail because they stopped believing in the value of a portal; they failed because they had the wrong mind-set. Their belief that they had revolutionized the Internet itself caused them to lose touch with what consumers truly valued. And this misconception proved to be their undoing.

If the executives of Yahoo! had focused instead upon understanding the changes in consumer behavior, and how they could best meet it, and how they had to adapt to better meet it in the future, they would never have missed their true value proposition as consumers saw it.

It is easy for executives to get so caught up in the changes that digital initiatives create that they fail to see their place within the market. Others fail to take these changes seriously enough, or to place proper value on information—information that can more accurately tell them their place in the market than ever before.

Amazon, on the other hand, was not thwarted by losing sight of true value or a desire to revolutionize the market. The company was created to give consumers something they always wanted: access to a vast catalogue of books from multiple publishers, and a customer-friendly, streamlined shopping experience where it was easy to find books they might be interested in. The Amazon team did an amazing job meeting this need. Within its first 30 days of business in 1995, Amazon sold books to people from all 50 US states and 45 different countries.

Jeff Bezos, the founder of Amazon, knew little about the book industry when he was tasked with researching new Internet-based business opportunities in the early 1990s.[9] As a computer science graduate of Princeton University, he understood computers and their potential. His research revealed that two large book publishers had their entire catalogs available in digital form, easily sharable via the web. He combined these two things—the catalogs and the Internet—to solve challenges that had long been obvious about the book industry: no physical bookstore could possibly carry even a fraction of the catalogs of major publishers, let alone every book available in print, and sourcing books directly from a publisher, without the need to distribute, display, and support a retail operation, would be significantly cheaper.

Bezos saw problems that had long plagued the book industry, problems that most people in the industry already knew. But what Bezos saw differently was a completely new, integrated approach to solving these old problems using the latest technology and techniques available. He used these to streamline supply chain operations, replacing the entire retail operations with a website; automated financial transactions; and used information to make the consumer book-selection process easier for the customer. He combined technology and physical process in a new way.

Because this had never been done before, and perhaps because of the astronomical success of Amazon, it is often said to have revolutionize the book industry, as if it created something new from nothing. But that is not what happened. Amazon did not change the inherent value proposition of the book industry or the reasons why consumers valued the products offered by it; Bezos kept his team focused upon their ability to meet this core value proposition. It was the unmoving stake in the ground around upon which everything else was built. And it could not have been changed even if Bezos tried. Consumers decide what they value. A company can either choose to satisfy it or fail in the process.

What Bezos actually did, after all of the hype surrounding his achievements is set aside, is help the book publishing and selling industry evolve to its next logical, more effective, and efficient model. He did not revolutionize it; he did not create something entirely new.

It is this focus on evolution—gradual, incremental change to a better form—and not a desire to revolutionize, that made Amazon successful. Starbucks displayed this evolutionary mind-set when it used a mobile application to vastly improve sales and operations at the point of maximum impact with its customers. Dunkin' Donuts had it when it used social media as a means to overcome a strategic weakness inherent in a franchise business model. The big-box retailer had it when it began using relationship status and big data to determine how it could drive incremental sales within a customer base of newly coupled consumers.

This mind-set focuses on the business' value proposition and doesn't allow the organization to become distracted by change. In an integrated enterprise, corporate leaders make sure that their subject-matter experts don't lose sight of the value proposition amid their excitement about creating social communities and building better mobile applications. These leaders make sure that everything flows from the value proposition, whether it's a new product, an improved service, or a digital strategy.

THE TECHNOLOGY-BUSINESS GAP

Integrated enterprises are brilliant at breaking down the barriers between information technology and the "business." Unfortunately, many organizations struggle to bridge the gap between technologists and business professionals themselves. This creates an obstacle for the integrated approach.

This gap can often be seen when companies try to implement new Enterprise Resource Planning applications. The technology integrators and functional managers have problems communicating with one another about how the applications should accommodate processes and what would be easiest for users. As a result, the implementation runs over schedule and over budget; functionality must be additionally revised; and management reports must be continuously rewritten. At the end of the implementation, management remains frustrated because they still can't answer the questions they were asking. This gap emanates from the inherently different language, training, and experience of these two groups. They see business differently.

This problem does not stem from IT personnel being technologists; the problem exists because most technologists are highly specialized subject-matter experts whereas most functional managers are generalists. Subject-matter experts most often operate as a support function and have a support mentality, whereas managers in charge of "the business" are directly responsible for business results. The goals set for subject-matter experts and managers are fundamentally different—one generates expense while the other generates revenue.

This gap between subject-matter experts and managers is an obstacle for every sizable organization, but it presents an even greater challenge as organizations attempt to move from a segregated approach to a fully integrated, Big Social Mobile enterprise. Each initiative—big data, social media, and mobile technology—requires an additional number of specialists. Each of these specialists speaks their own new language; each sees the business differently. Since these experts have little training, experience, or expertise in the core business functions within Sales or Operations, they have a mentality similar to technologists: they act as support functions, they set unique goals and measure success using metrics specific to their area. They think and often act in isolation.

This is commonly referred to as operating in silos. And much like a silo itself, these groups are vertically oriented. They must interact with those above them, and therefore are better at communicating vertically than horizontally. This dynamic is aided and reinforced because their boss often shares their background and understands them best. Big data, for example, typically falls under the larger IT department. Big data practitioners and IT professionals might not speak the exact same language, but they share much of one. This reinforces the silo mentality. Social media and mobile technology, while similar to big data, create an even more segmented, specialized mentality because they are relatively new specialties to most organizations. They do not share a language with any group that existed before they arrived. But they must report to someone, so social media is considered digital marketing and placed within Marketing, while mobile technology requires technical developers and is therefore put within the IT group. This too reinforces the silo mentality and keeps these functions disconnected from the larger organization.

When these specialized initiatives are segregated from the mainstream functions of the organization they rarely contribute to the success of the enterprise in any tangible way.

To overcome this obstacle to integration, organizations often consider using a matrix approach to connect these initiatives with other areas of the business.

A matrix structure does away with the traditional pyramid, hierarchical chain of command. It blends individuals with differing skill sets into working groups that lack clear reporting lines, allowing these groups to deal with issues of greater complexity and ambiguity. The common belief is that it does a better job of forcing mid-level managers to make more holistic decisions by exposing them to, and making them feel jointly responsible for, the success of a more diverse group of coworkers or subordinates from throughout the organization. Unfortunately, it is unlikely this will create the necessary integration.

While matrixes do often create more diverse management perspectives and theoretically might create synergies among diverse parts of the organization, they don't close the gap between subject-matter experts and business managers—at least not with regard to digital initiatives. If anything, the loose reporting structure can widen the gap, allowing managers to remain focused on the core business functions with which they are most familiar and believe to be most important, while social, mobile, and big data specialists flounder without any clear guidance or even self-direction. Matrix management does nothing to educate business people about how important these digital initiatives can be to the success of the enterprise, or even how they might be utilized. Nor does it educate these subject-matter experts on the company's business strategy, value proposition, or critical processes.

The only effective way to close the gap between these subject-matter experts and management—or more appropriately these digital initiatives and traditional business functions—is by using a definitive process that embeds big data, social media, and mobile technology into the enterprise itself. When this integration is effective, it shifts the corporate mind-set, allowing the company to then capitalize on these new capabilities. In fact, all of the obstacles discussed here can be overcome by people thinking differently about how these digital initiatives can and should be utilized. For many individuals, social and mobile are easily integrated into their personal lives, but this integration is more difficult in their professional lives.

Organizations need to shift their default perspective, and one catalyst that often creates this mental shift is recognizing that a major redefinition of consumers is in order—a redefinition we'll explore in the next chapter.

Chapter 4

UNDERSTANDING THE NEW SOCIAL CONSUMER

ORGANIZATIONS THAT GRASP THE CHANGING NATURE of consumers possess both the motivation and the insight to become Big Social Mobile. They know they can no longer interact with consumers the way they did in the past, recognizing that individuals have become much more diverse and much more powerful. Just as important, they realize how the consumer has changed and acknowledge the need for a more holistic, integrated approach that communicates with them more effectively.

Yet understanding the new social consumer is not as easy as it sounds. While every organizational leader understands that social communities and mobile technology have changed the essential nature of their markets and that new analytics offer tools to learn far more about these markets than previously possible, these leaders may still not "get it." They may not have the time or incentive to understand the true nature of this new social consumer. As a result, they see no reason or opportunity to embrace the integrated approach.

Recognizing how dramatically consumers have changed, however, can serve as the much-needed wake-up call.

REDEFINING THE CONSUMER

Today's consumers are smarter than they have ever been, utilizing social media and mobile technology as part of their decision-making process, and doing so in a way that gives them the most options at the lowest price. But these are only the superficial changes. The underlying evolution in consumer behavior is having a more significant impact upon how organizations structure and utilize the people, processes, information, and technologies that touch the consumer.

In the past, companies were able to identify who they cared about as either a customer or a prospect. Anyone that did not fall into one of these two categories was considered secondary or tangential; the broader market beyond these two groups was relatively unimportant to most companies.

Not anymore. Now almost anyone can affect a company's brand—positively and negatively.

As a result, organizations must cater to and care about a much broader group than just those individuals who generate revenue. This new definition of "customer" will certainly include traditional customers and prospects, but might also include social activists, organizational allies, suppliers, consultants, financial analysts, influential bloggers, and other social influencers in any corner of the world. Executives must think of their customer as any stakeholder who can influence the brand. Because this definition is broad, companies must now be concerned with two things:

- Creating a way to identify and communicate effectively and consistently with individual consumers.
- Creating a consistent way of interacting with the entire market that defines and reflects the company's attitude, opinions, and value proposition, and meets the expectations of all social consumers.

While this is a difficult task for companies who reflexively talk to customers from the narrow perspective of "what can I sell them," Big Social Mobile enterprises are motivated to understand today's consumer not only so that they can convert consumers to customers but also so that they can create an influential community attached to their brand—a community that will multiply its reach and influence and generate additional sales opportunities. The new social consumers are happy to do these things for brands they love and especially for companies that practice an integrated approach. These are organizations that can speak the language of the new consumer and speak it expertly across a diverse range of communication channels: social, mobile, and traditional websites, traditional and digital marketing, customer service and sales, product development, researchers or engineers, and even the executive management group.

THE VALUE OF CONNECTING

A consumer's choice to make a purchase, like a brand, or follow a company's social feed has implications beyond the action itself—implications for the consumer and for the company with which they choose to connect. They are making a public statement, something their friends and family will see posted on their social media pages, in their profile, and in the content they share. And for those friendships that they maintain exclusively in the digital world—long-lost friends from high school or college, ex-boyfriends or girlfriends that they still wish to secretly impress, even their professional peer group that they are competing against—these decisions will shape how they are perceived.

This may seem a foreign concept to some generations, but it is no different than the choice those Americans made in the 1950s when they decided to wear white T-shirts and leather jackets or sweaters and ties. The choice between being labeled a Greaser or a Soc defined an entire American generation. The car, or truck, or sport utility vehicle (SUV) people choose makes the same statement; their decision goes beyond just the functionality of the vehicle. Or do they refuse to buy a car at all, using only mass transit and bicycles to show the world how important the environment is to them?

In a way, this is nothing new; people have always made statements about themselves based on the brands and products they buy. Organizations usually grasp that they should align everything from the look of the product to the look of their logo with consumer preferences. Some companies learned that going even further could create greater loyalty with their consumer base—valet parking in front of exclusive retail locations, private shopping areas inside stores, or dedicated phone numbers and customer service agents for high-value clients.

Some companies, however, fail to recognize that they must adopt the same practices for social consumers across digital mediums. These segregated enterprises take one of two different approaches. Some define themselves with traditional processes—branding, marketing, sales, and operations—and then mimic the approach they use in these areas within each of their digital initiatives. They use content, campaigns, and processes designed to meet the needs of their traditional customers to appeal to today's social consumer. These companies find that they can sometimes build a community using these methods, but that they cannot effectively leverage that community. The community is not actively engaged; it only responds to simple offers of value such as coupons, discounts, or closeouts.

Other segregated organizations allow digital initiatives to operate as an island, creating the persona that they believe will best resonate with their digital community of social consumers. They may use standard company content, and their social feeds and mobile apps may have the same company logo at the top of each page, but everything that their community sees and experiences is filtered through social and mobile subject-matter-experts. If the brand is strong and the vision of the social and mobile practitioners resonates, these companies will create communities and can sometimes even leverage them, but success will always be limited. The problem is that when consumers interact with the company they see a disconnect between the social/mobile image and the organization's true beliefs and goals. Social practitioners may communicate that the company is doing everything possible to become a green organization, for example, but their business policies and practices may contradict the social propaganda. These companies then find themselves dealing with highly vocal, dissatisfied consumers posting negative comments and undermining the brand within their social circle. Their digital initiatives focus on damage control, and the digital community becomes transient; consumers come and go often.

Both of these segregated approaches suffer from a failure to internalize the consumer's perspective. Segregated companies adopt the platform but not the process. Facebook, Twitter, YouTube, LinkedIn, and any other social platform, in addition to the mobile apps that companies might create or allow themselves to become integrated into, are all valuable platforms for companies to leverage. But these are consumer platforms. For companies to use them effectively, they must use them in the same way the consumer does—as an extension of who they are, what they value, and the beliefs they hold dear.

The segregated approach does not extend the enterprise into the digital landscape; the social and mobile initiatives are not a true reflection of the company's culture and belief system. Integrated enterprises, on the other hand, are honest and transparent in the way they connect with social consumers. They make sure that every digital interaction reflects the company's mission and core values and that social and mobile subject-matter experts communicate this clearly and consistently.

Failing to connect with social consumers in this way is a huge mistake. Consider that 90 percent of people under the age of 30 use their smart phones first thing in the morning. Seventy-five percent of the time, they are checking their texts, email, and social feeds while they are still in bed. Forty-six percent of people do it while eating, and 33 percent while in the bathroom. And perhaps most surprisingly, 66 percent of people say they spend more time with their friends online than they do in person.[1] These individuals consciously evaluate the messages sent by organizations they like and follow, and if they sense a dissonance between what a social media expert tells them and what the company is really about, they will quickly become disengaged.

Only by integrating digital inititatives into the very core of the enterprise will companies be able to reflect the behavior that today's consumers place such high value upon, and demonstrate this each time the consumer interacts with them. Adopting this approach creates a lasting connection with the consumer.

THE POWER OF PASSION

Social consumers want to believe in as well as buy from *their* companies. They want to follow and do business with organizations whose values reflect their own. With a segregated approach, however, a company's values and beliefs rarely filter through to digital interactions. Because senior leadership and the heads of traditional departments are kept out of the digital loop, social consumers are usually not exposed to the people who shape the company's policies and practices. As a result, they don't feel as though they know the Chief Executive Officer (CEO) personally or see his or her commitment to solving social problems: food deserts in poor urban communities or the enlightened human resources (HR) policies that provide women with the flexibility to balance the demands of work and family.

Executives interact with consumers through a tightly controlled mixture of press releases, scripted interviews, and financial briefings, keeping as much information about their performance, their plans, and their problems as private as possible. They are the ones who create the company's culture and shape its values, but other employees create the actual connection. Leaving this connection to the social media and mobile experts, unfortunately, results in interactions that do little to energize and inspire most social consumers.

Today's consumers want open, honest communication; they want to know whether the belief system of the company aligns with their own. While consumers may still buy from the company and even remain loyal for a period of time, the connection between company and consumer is weak in segregated organizations. Without the emotional connection that comes from multiple interactions with a diverse group of managers and leaders, social consumers don't develop a vested interest in the company. Without this emotional connection, consumers are more easily swayed by other brands.

Integrated enterprises understand that they must facilitate online communication between organizational leaders and social consumers. The goal is not just to let leaders tell consumers what they believe in but to find out what's important to consumers and factor that into corporate strategy and culture. Social consumers look at the entire performance and policies of a company, not just the value of its individual products and services, before they emotionally commit.

Amilcar Perez, vice president (VP) of Marketing for The Nielsen Company, speaks to this point in a recent report that reflects that 8 out of 10 of the world's Internet users—today's social consumers—believe that it is important for companies to implement programs that benefit the environment or society: "A global social conscience is one of the biggest trends to have emerged in the last decade. Globalization, the media and rapid penetration of the Internet have turned key international social and political issues into personal issues. From human rights to poverty and war, and most significantly, the environment— global consumers are collectively speaking out and demanding that corporations make a positive contribution to society."[2]

It may seem challenging to integrate this type of consumer mind-set into the modern day processes of a corporation, but it is possible. For instance, a publically traded software company made a decision to interact with the market in a much different way than the traditional segregated enterprise. The management team decided to remove the barrier between their executive group and the consumer, so that they could build the type of meaningful, personal relationship that their customers, potential customers, and social influencers were looking for.

While Christian, the CEO of this software company, was gearing up for the quarterly financial analyst briefing, his Chief Marketing Officer commented on recent studies that showed it was financially advantageous for companies to link themselves with social or environmental issues. This spurred a discussion about various social issues that the senior management team believed they should take a stand on.

During this meeting, the management team agreed that they needed to do a better job of turning their beliefs about social issues into programs and let people outside of the company know where they stood. Many of the people in the room, including Christian, were concerned about the growing problem of homelessness in their area and decided to help combat it. Christian mentioned his company's new activism program during the financial analyst briefing and it went largely unnoticed. He then told the young man in charge of the company's social media initiative to post news about the program on their social feed. Almost instantly, it became the most popular post in company history. Followers wanted to know what this commitment meant in concrete terms.

Christian met with his senior managers and then the three employees in his social media department and eventually decided that he himself would post a series of explanations about the company's efforts on their social feeds, under his own name, in his own words. He would respond to comments whenever possible or through his social media staff if he couldn't.

Consumer engagement increased instantly, both within their community and among bloggers, writers and other industry experts. The company continued its normal practice of posting news about their products and services and found there was a spillover effect; engagement continued to increase. As Christian noted to his staff, the community had become "supercharged; our passion became their passion."

At the next quarterly analyst briefing, Christian decided to run the meeting as usual, but also decided to record it and make it publically available. In addition, Christian would then run another briefing session for the social influencers in their community—those people who had become most engaged on the topic of their new program. It would be conducted like an interview with questions from their public feed, so that he could answer on the spot, without preparation.

Christian said he was surprised at the outcome of the two-hour social influencer briefing. He had expected most of the questions to be about the new programs to help the homeless, and some were, but the majority were about where the company was going strategically, what new products they would launch, and what they expected the financial impact would be—and why they were making these decisions. Christian couldn't answer some specific questions because they would reveal too much information to competitors, but he answered most of them, providing insight about his leadership team's decision-making process.

The entire community—financial analysts included—responded positively to Christian's efforts. They were aware of the social media buzz that resulted from Christian's attempt to make sure his team was involved in and honest about their communication through social channels. The directness and sincerity of Christian's interaction in the social influencer briefing impressed analysts, as did the way the discussion broadened to a range of other business topics. They could see that Christian was connecting with his online audience, and they saw his leadership in this area as one additional reason to recommend the company.

The company's valuation improved significantly.

Since the value of a company is largely influenced by a prediction of future performance, not its actual past financial performance (as many people falsely assume), the better information analysts and consumers have—especially information that is coming unfiltered, in near real-time directly from senior executives—the more confidence they have in their prediction. This is reflected in stock performance, with companies that have a strong customer focus out-performing the market on cumulative return by 28.5 percentage points, while companies without this focus average 33.9 points less than the market average.[3] Christian had discovered that there was a tangible value in their new transparency.

Social consumers, whether they know it or not, are highly influenced by their emotional connection to a brand: the greater the passion, the greater the connection, the greater their commitment. This connection has a tangible financial value, since a significant percentage of these highly engaged consumers are likely to become loyal, long-term customers. In turn, these passionate individuals will aid the company in growing the social community and bringing in new customers; they also are more willing to aid the company in understanding their place in the market, their differentiators, and how they might improve products and even internal processes.

A passionate connection with consumers has always been powerful, but it was traditionally created only by lifestyle brands—brands whose popularity was driven by the interests, beliefs, or attitude of a definable group. Consumers were passionate about brands such as Apple or Rolex years before social and mobile came into existence, but they weren't more likely to actively engage with these brands. They were passionate because the brand image dovetailed with their own self-image. The connection established by companies like Christian's runs much deeper. When a company's digital persona reflects its beliefs and is integrated into processes, policies, and procedures consistent with these beliefs, it creates passion. Big Social Mobile enterprises communicate in a way that is authentic and meets the social consumers' desire for authenticity. This doesn't mean that leaders like Christian have to engage directly with consumers via social and mobile media all the time, but it shows that allowing a diverse group of decision makers from throughout the organization to interact directly with consumers has a positive effect. These leaders often understand *why* processes or policies are put in place, why a product was designed the way it was, or even why the company's social policy is the way it is.

SPEAKING THE CONSUMER'S LANGUAGE

Consumers are used to existing within a community that includes family and friends, coworkers, casual acquaintances, and people with whom they share interests. These individuals understand them, speak their language and can therefore influence the decisions they make—not just big life decisions, but also small day-to-day ones, such as what clothes to buy, what concerts to see, or which products will make them happiest.

Companies are used to being included in this social circle and being part of the customer's decision making process. They didn't have to do much more than provide good products at a fair price, offer reasonable service, and be easily accessible (either online or through a convenient physical location) in order to make consumers feel like they were necessary. But, unfortunately for companies, this has changed. No longer is convenience, price, or even satisfactory service the primary driver of customer loyalty or consumer purchasing. The new social consumer needs more—they need to feel a passionate connection to the brand and believe that an organization is speaking their language before they commit. And they are willing to incur a bit more expense (driving a little farther or paying slightly more) to get it. This does not mean they will not ever purchase from companies with whom they do not feel these things, but rather that they will select the company to which they feel most connected whenever there is an option.

Companies that continue to use traditional approaches—most of which are the digital equivalent of push marketing (who shouts the loudest and the most frequently)—will find themselves excluded from the consumer's social circle. The result is a missed opportunity, and less revenue or profit than they might otherwise have generated. Big Social Mobile enterprises have learned to communicate and operate in ways that makes them feel more than just necessary to consumers. They speak the consumer's language and this earns them a place in the consumer's social circle.

Consider that the most accepted empirical study puts the average attention span of a person that frequently uses the Internet as having dropped from 12 seconds, in 2000, to 8 seconds in 2008—less than the average attention span of a goldfish. Consider, too, that 25 percent of teens forget major details of close friends and relatives and 7 percent of people forget their own birthdays. We're bombarded with information, we're busier than ever before, and consequently, we're remembering less. Traditional branding, which relied upon memorable marketing campaigns so that the consumer recalled the brand at their moment of need, are becoming increasingly less effective as consumers retain less information.

Even more significant, communications across the digital landscape—web, social, or mobile—have shifted from content posted in status updates, or simple text-based posts, to linking these posts to articles, to posts using pictures for content, and finally to video posts. Today, the only medium consumed via the Internet capable of holding the attention span of consumers is video, with an average viewing time of 2.7 minutes (it is important to note that this number is skewed by the influence of web-based television, which typically runs longer than advertisements). While watching a video, the average office worker will have checked his email five times.[4] But even video is falling prey to a drop in consumer attention span. The new YouTube venture, MixBit, limits videos to 16 seconds, a full 10 seconds longer than Vine allows, and 1 second longer than Instagram allows.

This creates obvious problems for companies trying to connect with consumers and speak their language. Video is now the most effective medium to create tangible results within digital sales channels: retail site visitors who view video stay two minutes longer on average and are 64 percent more likely to make a purchase than other site visitors. Marketers who use video in email cite increased click-through rates, increased time spent reading the email, increased sharing and forwarding, increased conversion rates, and increased dollars generated as the top benefits and visitors who view product videos are 85 percent more likely to buy than visitors who do not.[5]

At the same time, only one out of four marketers uses video in email campaigns, with 43 percent of marketers citing a lack of available video content as their reason for not using video in email campaigns. This shows how, despite the widespread acknowledgment that video is the format of the future, few social and mobile initiatives have access to the resources necessary to create video content. Therefore further integration between an organization and its social media programs is required. Not only must these initiatives be integrated into core processes (so that valuable content is created), they must also be integrated into the content creation process itself—the processes that actually create print, digital, video, and multimedia content—while this content is being created, not after the fact. Moreover, consumer demands are constantly changing, and the content creation process must be flexible enough to take these changes into account, so that this content will actually attract their attention.

Making it even more challenging for companies to connect with consumers, social and mobile consumers don't read everything that companies post. The average Internet website page contains 593 words. Digital consumers read only 28 percent of them, and stay on that page less than four seconds 17 percent of the time.[6] Although difficult to calculate, the average number of words read on a webpage is approximately 50 words.

Given short attention spans and the tendency to read a relatively small percentage of what companies post, the right people must communicate the right information. Unfortunately, social and mobile practitioners are usually in charge of adapting sales and marketing language to short, digital bursts, and the most valuable part of the message can get mangled in the process. Leaders, managers, sales people, and even perhaps traditional marketing professionals understand and have deep experience communicating the value proposition of the company. These experts can create language that has a positive impact on social consumers. Social and mobile practitioners may be skilled at boiling the message down to 140 characters, but they lack the insight and experience to ensure it's a message that reflects the organization's key principles and responds to consumer concerns and expectations.

A sure sign of a segregated approach is substituting entertainment value for a clear, compelling statement that consumers "get." Cool mobile applications and funny videos are fine, but this isn't what social consumers want as much as a company that understands what matters to them, why they are interested in the company, and what they need from the company (information, ideas, decisions, processes, functionality, feedback). Big Social Mobile enterprises understand what social consumers are looking for, and by speaking honestly, perceptively, and helpfully—in the language of the target audience group—they motivate consumers to become loyal, long-term customers.

THE CONSUMER'S DEFINITION OF VALUE

Segregated companies provide social and mobile consumers with a basic level of value. They can entertain, answer questions, and supply information—all basic and necessary things. However, this does not equate to what social consumers now define as value or valuable. For them, value means content that has a meaningful impact on their purchasing decisions and even on their lives. They expect companies to draw upon their vast resources and tap into their expertise to give them something that they could not obtain on their own. Integrated organizations can do this because the interactions they have with consumers are connected to all corporate sectors. The right information flows from the right source to the right consumer at the right time.

You would think that after ten years of trying to capture the attention of social consumers on a wide variety of platforms, all companies would be aware of this more advanced definition of value. This definition, though, remains a moving target. As companies evolve to become more effective on a changing digital landscape, consumers are also changing as they react to new technologies, platforms, and approaches. They are incrementally redefining what value means to them, and no doubt, the definition will change in the future.

The consumer's definition of value, as interpreted by executives, influences all of the activities that employees are tasked to perform, either in concert or isolation. If these leaders believe that consumers still define value in the most basic of ways, then they will see no reason to create truly meaningful content—or, by extension, to become a Big Social Mobile enterprise capable of consistently producing and delivering high-value content.

Typically, here's how segregated companies approach digital initiatives based on their limited interpretation of what consumers will find valuable:

- It must be social, and therefore companies become involved on the social platforms that accommodate this.
- It must be entertaining, and therefore companies attempt to share or create content that is funny, interesting, or at least attention-grabbing.
- It must be a routine part of the consumer's life, which is accomplished through the widespread adoption of mobile technology and the availability of social platforms on mobile devices, or through mobile applications that the company creates.

*   *   *

Enlightened social and mobile practitioners take these four requirements one step further. They talk about the ratio of purely entertaining messages delivered via social platforms or mobile devices versus those that are clearly sales-oriented and designed to prompt a purchase. And they talk about how their digital initiatives must be personal, showing that companies are paying attention to consumers, can communicate effectively with them one-on-one, and allowing them to voice their opinions and complaints.

The Big Social Mobile mind-set goes even further, making these discussions meaningful, ensuring that the most current consumer definition of value is addressed. Integrated enterprises measure the success of their social and mobile corporate-consumer interactions in terms of their ability to increase revenue, reduce expense, and improve profitability, and things that directly drive these ultimate measures of business. Consequently, they must give social and mobile consumers more than funny videos. Is there real value in entertaining the consumer for entertainment purposes alone? No, not when viewed through the profit lens. Will this entertainment further the purposes of the company, even something as nebulous as maintaining a connection with the consumer so that they can be marketed to? No, because there are too many other sources of entertainment. Even companies whose sole purpose is to provide social entertainment for the consumer must provide more than just entertainment to create any real connection.

Consider MySpace. Both MySpace and Facebook met the same basic need for consumers: they both provided an entertaining social platform through which users could interact with their social community. MySpace empha-sized customizable home pages, blog-like user posts, and photographs while Facebook emphasized personal connections and interactions, but their core value proposition was the same.

The Internet wasn't big enough for two mega-brand social networks. One of them had to go. From its creation in 2003, it took MySpace exactly eight years to become the number one social platform, to be toppled from that place by Facebook, enact massive layoffs, and be sold at a relatively discounted price.[7] MySpace still exists, but no one you know uses it.

MySpace failed for many reasons—namely a poor corporate take-over, pressure to produce revenue before social media was mature, and a lack of innovation—but its primary reason for failure was not keeping up with the changing definition of what consumers found valuable. As consumers began to fully understand the potential of social media their opinion about how these two platforms facilitated social interaction changed. While MySpace was focusing its resources on designing functionality that enabled direct market-ing to generate revenue from its community, Facebook focused on enabling greater social interaction within its community. Consumers responded.

Facebook and numerous other success stories demonstrate how consumers value information and interactivity that they would otherwise not have access to above anything else. For Facebook this was social interaction—and then social interaction tied to direct marketing. What consumers valued came first.

All companies are the experts on their products and services. They know how to use them most effectively or in ways that consumers might not have thought of. They know where the consumer can find them most easily, at the cheapest price. They also understand industry trends, research, and events that the consumer might find useful. They are gathering houses for information that customers and potential customers wish they had access to.

Integrated enterprises don't limit themselves to dispensing sales and mar-keting information but broaden their role to include sharing information that will make the lives of those in their social communities better. They can share how other consumers are using their products and services in new and creative ways—ways they might not even have thought of themselves. They can share their insights into the bigger issues, tying the discussion into the social con-sciousness of their community to create more passion or to promote the latest news stories, providing value-added insights or perspectives.

Consumers may also value how the company itself operates, makes decisions, and creates policy, from multiple perspectives inside the organization. Followers often relish gaining access to an executive or a technologist, or seeing the CEO debate a company's products, services, processes, place in the market, or social policy. That's interesting. That's something people will follow and engage in. That's a community consumers want to be part of and a company they want to support. Big Social Mobile enterprises possess the capacity to quickly channel all of their expertise to consumers to create this type of engagement.

This approach still accommodates the same three basic rules of digital social interaction—it must be social, entertaining, and routine—and it also accommodates the things that more progressive social and mobile practitioners are focused on—making it personal and balancing marketing versus value—but does so in a way that makes the company irreplaceable. This does not mean that companies should never post content that is purely entertaining and is only tangentially related to their brand or industry. This content is important; it is fun. But it is only filler. If it comprises the majority of content an organization is delivering via social or mobile, mixed in with the occasional sales pitch, then the company is not creating real value in the eyes of the consumer. When the consumer finds something more entertaining, or when the consumer finds another company that can meet their needs while delivering this truly valuable content, they will quickly spend their valuable, limited time with this competitor.

COMPETING FOR THE CONSUMER

Social, mobile, and big data subject-matter experts often fail to think in competitive terms. These specialists focus on building communities without understanding that they are actually vying for a highly prized commodity in today's social economy: time. The consumer's time.

An increasing number of companies, platforms, applications, and technology are clamoring for consumers' attention. These specialists understand that engagement is key, but they often don't grasp how to secure this engagement in a highly competitive environment where their failure equals a competitor's gain. They also don't grasp that their digital initiatives are vying against many other digital efforts for not only a dwindling supply of consumers' time but also a fixed amount of revenue generated by each consumer throughout their lifetime.

Talking about the competition for time isn't semantics. Consider that not only do consumers struggle to find time for multiple social platforms—as MySpace learned—but they also only have a limited amount of usable space on the first screen of their smart phone or tablet, the favorite's bar of their web browser, the top half of their favorite's menu, or key positions on their computer desktop; they will only allow a small number of companies to clutter their social news feeds. The companies that make themselves valuable enough to earn these top spots are also most likely to earn a larger percentage of the consumer's mindshare and wallet-share.

If you possess an integrated mind-set—if you view the digital landscape as connected to the bricks-and-mortal environment—then you probably understand the fierce competition for social consumers' time. Shelf space, end caps, high traffic areas, and eye-level shelves are highly prized and highly analyzed locations for companies that sell their products via retailers. The measures of their performance abound: volume, revenue, and margin per placement and linear foot, number of facings, foot traffic, and velocity. On the Internet, similar analysis is done on banner placements, key words, and ad words, and a significant amount of money is spent to ensure the highest ranking in search engines because that means more eyeballs and higher click-through rates. The value of Internet real estate even follows the ancient mantra: location, location, location. The most common words with a .com extension are worth the most money when sold as domain names.

Smart phone users check their phone on average of 150 times per day, or approximately once every 10 minutes. If you subtract time spent sleeping, this number is closer to once every six minutes.[8] If companies were truly conscious of the competition for consumers' time, they would create measures for the company's ability to secure and utilize these highly trafficked social consumer locations.

Unfortunately, many otherwise smart executives and digital subject-matter experts don't think in these terms for two reasons. First, this is an entirely new thought process for them. Only the most progressive Big Social Mobile enterprises can use traditional methods of measurement across the digital landscape, such as those that actually quantify the value of a specific social influencer or the margin of a customer that originated via social media. Second, the answers are contained in big data, not traditional enterprise data. Only integrated enterprises have taken the time to blend these two different and disparate data sets into one view that seamlessly reflects performance and profit across both the physical and digital landscapes. This allows management to see the connection between what has traditionally driven the success of their enterprise and how this corresponds with consumer behavior in the digital space.

Companies that make these connections train their big, social, and mobile experts to think in competitive terms and integrate them into the functions of the enterprise. As a result, these experts see digital performance in the same terms as the traditional drivers of performance in the physical world. These experts understand big data and consumer behavior from an integrated perspective. Their role is not to act as islands within the enterprise but as bridges between the modern consumer and traditional management—the latter group investing heavily in these digital initiatives individually but still seeking to realize the returns that only integration can provide.

Perhaps most important of all, Big Social Mobile enterprises understand the decision-making process that results in a purchase far better than their more segregated competitors. They have a grasp of the process in which the consumer is seamlessly transitioning from the physical world to the digital world and back, over and over. When consumers decide they want or need a product they search the web to see what their options are and where it is available. Sometimes they go to the physical location. And when they are there they search competitive information and pricing on their mobile device. Armed with this knowledge they talk to a salesperson about the added benefits of one product versus another or additional discounts. They fact check this information online while in-store and review the company's social media presence, sometimes watching videos about the product. They post questions on social media to solicit the advice of their friends. After the purchase they register it online, they post their opinion, and they check for social and mobile feeds relative to it as they drive home.

Consumers have removed the barrier between the physical and digital worlds. They live in both simultaneously, rapidly, and fluidly transitioning from one to the other. To take advantage of these new behaviors, organizations must broaden and deepen their view of these social consumers. They must design integrated processes and measures that take these behaviors into consideration. This can only be done if social and mobile practitioners are routinely interacting with marketing, sales and other core business functions (and in some cases supporting functions), and only if these new behaviors of today's social consumer are integrated into corporate strategy.

Part II

CREATING A BIG SOCIAL MOBILE ENTERPRISE

MOST LEADERS CAN ASSESS THE CONSUMER standing in front of them, gauge their mood by the tone of their voice or the length of a pause, and estimate the likelihood of them becoming a customer. They need to become just as adept at assessing today's social consumer in the same way—despite their lack of physical presence.

At the heart of what makes an organization Big Social Mobile is the way digital initiatives are woven into its fabric—the way all people, processes, technology, and information work together to provide one consistent view of consumer demographics and behavior across both physical and digital landscapes. This view allows executives, managers, and employees at all levels of an organization to give consumers a uniform experience regardless of which medium, channel, or portion of the enterprise they are interacting with (sometimes called an "omni-channel" experience). Integrating big data, social media, and mobile technology fully into the organization also provides leaders with insight into larger, long-term trends or changes in expectations. All levels and functions throughout the organization are ready to engage consumers so that each interaction creates greater attachment between the consumer and the organization, while also influencing them to exhibiting the behaviors that the organization seeks. This means that not only can organizations maximize the value of each interaction, but also that they can proactively or intentionally control or manipulate consumer behavior (what is sometimes called "predictive marketing").

Most organizational leaders believe in this ideal—the idea of becoming Big Social Mobile, but they always ask one question: How? The methodology described in this section aims to provide a step-by-step understanding of the skills necessary to operate in an integrated fashion. To provide context on where these steps will be taking you, an overview of the process is provided here:

1. Understanding Digital Relationships: Segmenting your current communities into five different types of digital relationships—customers, prospects, influencers, partners and competitors—to understand how each can be best leveraged.

2. Defining Customer and Consumer Interactions: Detailing the interactions that your organization is having with customers and consumers in both the physical and digital worlds, from the moment you first meet them until they stop interacting with your organization.

3. Identifying Ideal Digital Behaviors: Defining how your organization would prefer to interact with consumers and customers, and how you would prefer them to behave so that their behavior is leading to the highest conversion rate, the lowest costs, the highest revenue per

customer; and being able to position them for add-on/up-sales, the highest customer lifetime value, and other tangible benefits.

4. Analyzing Profitable Patterns and Segments: Understanding how the gap between current interactions and ideal interactions can be closed using five different types of analysis—behavioral, social, geospatial, device, and financial—and how this analysis helps sub-segment your organization's communities to identify perfect customers and promote ideal behaviors.

5. Aligning Digital Initiatives with the Enterprise: Creating the right organizational structure that integrates all of the skills and processes necessary to achieve the Big Social Mobile ideal into your organization's people, process, technology,and information; facilitating the right behaviors among your community, interacting with social consumers in the way that they prefer, and providing a consistent consumer experience across all channels.

*   *   *

Many organizations have already launched segregated initiatives that have created communities, collected data, and developed mobile applications. The process here can be used to bring existing but segregated initiatives into the enterprise core. Although the process is laid out as linear steps for the sake of easy comprehension, these steps are not nearly so linear in real life. Instead, they may be implemented simultaneously, reiteratively, and with greater emphasis on one step than another depending on an organization's particular issues. Putting the process into practice requires testing, assessment, and exploration, helping management continuously improve their effectiveness at interacting with consumers across both the physical and digital landscape.

Put another way, this process is designed to help you gain an incremental understanding of your customers and the social consumers within it, expanding your knowledge to consumers you interact with and the market as a whole, to uncover new consumers and segments that can be sold to. Eventually, the process will help you transition to a perspective where you are seeking to not only to understand but also to control interactions. This will allow your organization to adapt its processes so that they solicit ideal behaviors and responses from your customers and consumers, maximizing your results.

Chapter 5

UNDERSTANDING DIGITAL RELATIONSHIPS

EVERY COMPANY CREATES A STRATEGIC PLAN designed to do one simple thing: turn consumers into customers. From this simple beginning spring complex strategic objectives, financial projections, management teams, and then knowledge workers and supporting personnel. A set of processes weave these together so that they can gather or create the tangible assets, both physical and digital, necessary to identify, influence, and convert consumers to customers. All activities within the enterprise must participate in the creation of profit. And profit can only be created in one of very few ways: by obtaining new customers, by convincing current customers to purchase more, or by reducing the expense associated with these efforts. Even departments that seem to have little positive impact on the profit equation can be tied back to it. HR provides the necessary people to perform the tasks that create profit and seeks to constantly increase the collective skills and capabilities of the organization. Legal seeks to negotiate to the company's best advantage and protect it from revenue-draining lawsuits. Improvement efforts, such as Lean or Six Sigma, seek to help the organization operate more effectively and efficiently.

Big data, social media, and mobile technology must be held to these same standards.

To adhere to these standards, organizations must analyze the digital relationships that these initiatives are creating. When companies understand where they stand relative to key groups within their social communities, they are in a much better position to integrate their big, social, and mobile efforts into their core, profit-making strategy. To grasp the value of analyzing digital relationships, let's look at a recent example from the accounting industry.

ACCOUNTING COMES OF AGE

Analyzing digital relationships and combining this analysis with the broader definition of what a "customer" is helps create different subsegments within a company's social community that can be used in different ways, each to the company's best advantage. This is particularly important within an industry that is fully saturated and highly competitive, such as the accounting industry; within this industry, every consumer that needs an accountant already has one. To make matters worse, technology-driven solutions entered this market over a decade ago, undermining the traditional relationship-based model where an account works one-on-one with clients to prepare their taxes.

These technology-driven solutions (where a person answers narrative questions) at first gained little traction because companies couldn't anticipate the wide range of questions and information people required before they felt comfortable answering tax-related questions. While this technology could complete annual tax returns at a fraction of the cost of a real accountant, customers were dissatisfied. It could not bring the same people back year-after-year, improving customer lifetime value, the meaningful metric for software-based solutions.

Seeking to find a better approach that still relied on technology, one company in this industry added Customer Service Agents who would be available to the customer base via email, website submissions, and eventually online chat. These highly trained agents would be able to respond to specific customer questions. But this solution was unsustainable; it was too expensive.

In response to this, a competing firm analyzed the relationships they had within their social communities—their digital relationships—and discovered that on their social feed (where customers often posted tax-related questions) a number of people within their community were providing answers to people's questions. Their feed was monitored and managed by a low-level marketing person with no accounting experience.

During the break before the next tax season, this company revised its software to include direct access to a social feed that they would monitor and manage. They also provided direct links and search functionality to a knowledge base where customers could pose specific questions. At the same time they identified those individuals within their community who responded most frequently, focusing on their degree of accuracy and average response time. They learned that these people were providing consistently sound advice and responding more quickly than their own Customer Service professionals. Additional research revealed that some of these community respondents were certified public accounts and that they shared certain demographics—most of them were older, retired accountants who were answering the questions as part of their online social activities and because it allowed them to continue to use their hard-won knowledge in useful ways.

They invited these "community experts" to become VIP community members, gave them software that allowed them to oversee the social feed and knowledge manager, created special profiles for them, and ran a competition among them, awarding significant prizes based upon accuracy, response time, and the number of answers they provided. This firm also advertised their VIP advice feature, driving people toward their social community and capitalizing on consumer frustration with other online accounting services. Every performance metric moved in the right direction: new customers, returning customers, customer satisfaction, and market share. In one year the firm was able to integrate social media and big data into the core function of its enterprise, operations, and software solutions; create a competitive advantage; and help the software-based accounting industry evolve to its next, better form.

This firm is an example of a company that analyzed its digital relationships and reaped competitive advantage as a result. Rather than allowing their social initiatives to languish within the segregated confines of their social media experts, they broadened the scope of this initiative so that a cross-section of their organization was involved in the effort. This is the first, crucial step of integration—looking closely at the relationships you have within your social communities.

Let's examine how to analyze each of the five types of digital relationships (see Figure 5.1):

- Digital customers
- Digital prospects
- Social influencers
- Partners
- Competitors

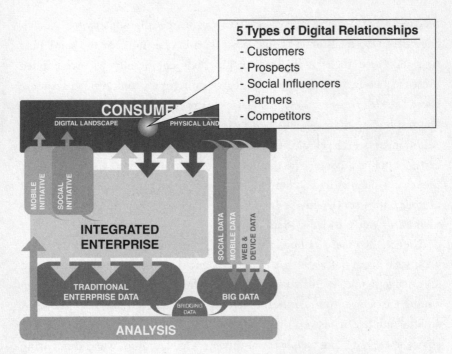

5 Types of Digital Relationships

- Customers
- Prospects
- Social Influencers
- Partners
- Competitors

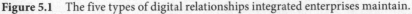

Figure 5.1   The five types of digital relationships integrated enterprises maintain.

DIGITAL CUSTOMERS

Digital customers come in many forms. They place orders via websites, customer service centers, email, phone, or even physical storefronts. In all of these cases, they leave a digital fingerprint in an order entry system, an ecommerce website, a loyalty program, or another application designed to facilitate this transaction. The social or mobile initiatives of a company may also facilitate these transactions and leave similar fingerprints. Each company will have a variety of channels, some of which generate actual customers and some of which do not, but in all cases the company knows exactly who they are and what they have purchased.

These customers can be leveraged by the company in many ways, both at a macro-level, with techniques such as broadcast marketing (sometimes called "batch & blast" campaigns) and at a micro-level, with tailored emails or micro-marketing, SMS messages, traditional mail, or even phone calls—because the company knows exactly who they are.

Categorizing Consumers
(logical hierarchy)

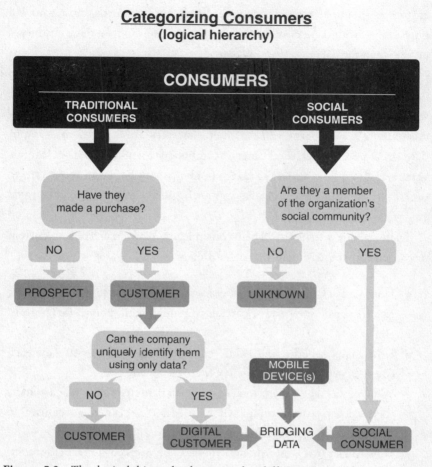

Figure 5.2 The logical hierarchy between the different types of relationships integrated enterprises maintain and how they are categorized.

Customers that can be uniquely identified using *only* their data are considered "digital customers." Conversly, if a customer cannot be uniquely identified using only their data they should not be considered digital customers. Every organization will have many customers, only some of which are digital customers who can be leveraged using Big Social Mobile techniques [See Figure 5.2].

This distinction is important because it has a real world impact. For example, employees working for companies in physical locations, such as retail outlets or restaurants, often know high-value customers by sight, either because they see these customers more frequently or because the greater amount of money they spend causes employees to make a mental note. These employees know these customers should be treated differently. But, other employees, those who will only interact with these customers digitally, only know to treat these customers differently if the data tells them.

Therefore, being able to determine who a consumer is based solely upon data holds special significance within Big Social Mobile enterprises. Leaders within these organizations understand that their digital initiatives can only create greater long term value if their processes are adapted to accomodate these needs (such as the need to uniquely identify digital customers whenever possible). While these requirements may not seem important to organizations using a segregated approach, they are critical to integrated enterprises.

These specific questions will help you understand how many of your current or past customer are actually digital customers:

- How many channels does your company have that generates customers? Retail, websites, partners, partner websites, email, phone, fax, portals, etc.
- How many specific, individual customers can you identify for each channel? And when were each of these customers gained?
- What percentage of your total customers are therefore digital customers (because they can be uniquely identified)? What can you organization do to increase this percentage?
- How robust is the information you have on each customer? How complete, how accurate, and how up-to-date? If you wanted to reach out and have a meaningful conversation with this customer, how helpful would this information be?

The example of how high-value customers are treated differently from average customers shows that all customers—whether digitally identifiable or not—are not created equal.

Some customers, those who can be thought of as traditional customers (people who have not yet become social consumers), interact with the company because they need or want the company's products or services. They might reference online reviews that give them insight into how to return a product or reach customer service if they have a problem, but they do not care about the company itself. These customers take from the company without giving, or rather, they give only revenue in exchange for goods or service. The relationship ends there.

Other customers—ones who arrive and/or stay connected via social media and mobile technology—feel a connection to the company itself and often believe they are building a lasting connection. These are the most passionate group of consumers associated with the brand. Whereas traditional customers care only about what is in it for them, social consumers view the transaction as part of a larger, longer-term relationship. As such, they are willing to help the company in many ways. They are willing to invest more than just revenue into the relationship. The distinction between traditional customers and social consumers is just as important, and just as fundamental, to Big Social Mobile enterprises as is the distrinction between digital and nondigital customers.

These distinctions are more than nuance; they are behavioral. When researching the Customer Service performance of a company, a traditional customer asks: Will I be able to get good service if I need it? A social consumer asks: Do I want to be associated with a brand that offers this type of service to its customers? The traditional value proposition of the company still retains a powerful influence over this social consumer, but social consumers are willing to allow additional factors beyond just the base value of a product or service to influence their propensity to buy. These customers—social consumers who become customers—are the lifeblood of the Big Social Mobile enterprise.

Companies can separate their digital customers into two groups, traditional customers and social consumers, through a simple process. Traditional customers (who are digital customers) leave a clear data trail through traditional sales channels (retail, direct sales, customer service order entry, or ecommerce, for example). These customers are identifiable in the central Enterprise Resource Planning application because they ordered and received a product or service at some point in the past. They may also be contained in Customer Relationship Management software or normalized within larger data stores or data warehouses.

During the process of becoming a customer, many customers will have given the company their email address or their phone number at the time of purchase (or through a more complicated process of purchasing and joining a loyalty program at the same time). Most companies already capture these items as part of the purchasing process or transaction. These two data points are the most common "bridge" between consumers as they exist in the physical world and their profiles in the digital world—their social and mobile profiles.

In segregated enterprises, however, these bridges lead nowhere. The company cannot directly connect the customer (whose information is contained within traditional enterprise data) to any social or mobile profile (contained in big data); the company does not know anything about the social or mobile behavior of customers and can find no trace of them in the information they glean from big data. While these customers have created a digital copy of themselves during the sales transaction, the connections that are at the heart of Big Social Mobile enterprises don't exist in segregated organizations. As a result, these customers cannot be identified as social consumers and therefore cannot be leveraged.

Within integrated enterprises, these same customers, through these two key data points and others, can be directly connected to one or more of their social profiles. This connection allows the company to track and analyze the behavior of these physical customers across the digital landscape. They leave a trail of big data behind them that can be used to specifically identify and target them, to influence them, and to interact with them.

Some companies can clearly identify every customer they have ever done business with—their traditional customer base. They can also identify the people they are interacting with through any number of social or mobile platforms. But they cannot connect the two. Without this ability, they can never become truly Big Social Mobile.

This then becomes the first step of becoming Big Social Mobile: separating customers that can be leveraged as social consumers from those who cannot.

You can facilitate this analysis by taking the following actions:

- Determine how many uniquely identifiable digital customers have records containing *bridging data* such as phone numbers and email addresses.
- Assess whether these identifiable customers' records also contain social or mobile identifiers or profile names; calculate the percentage of customers who can also be identified as social consumers.
- Identify the number of different mobile applications or social media platforms that can be identified using this customer data and how many customers are identified on each.
- Connect these customers to information about them contained within big data that the company gathers.

If your company has adopted a segregated approach, it's likely you will struggle to take these actions and that a very low percentage of your company's digital customers can also be identified as social consumers.

Most segregated organizations initially concentrate their social and mobile efforts on building as big a community as possible as quickly as possible. They then encourage their community to engage with the brand. While this creates a community that can be leveraged, it cannot be fully leveraged until community members (and their relationship to organization) can be uniquely identified (because techniques such as micro-marketing, predictive marketing and personalized interactions rely upon this understanding to be effective). By identifying and understanding each customer, the company will be able to take the next step in the process of becoming Big Social Mobile: understanding how your organization is interacting with each consumer in order to maximize the tangible benefits.

This approach also creates the proper mind-set for everyone within the organization. It connects them to the primary goal of the enterprise itself: generating customers to maximize profit. Integrated enterprises use all of their assets and all of their channels to achieve this goal, social and mobile being just two. Starting with this focus clearly lets the organization know that all of its efforts—digital initiatives included—must contribute to organizational objectives in meaningful, tangible ways. For those in charge of digital initiatives it clearly says that creating friends, followers, and even engagement (while important and worthwhile) is not the primary goal—creating customers is.

DIGITAL PROSPECTS

Just as customers who can be digitally identified as social consumers are more valuable to the enterprise than unidentifiable or traditional customers, digital prospects who can be identified as social consumers also possess the same higher value. Big Social Mobile enterprises recognize this value, not just because these prospects are more easily converted to customers—more valuable customers—but because they too can be used in creative ways to assist the organization.

The process of identifying these prospects is similar to that of identifying social consumers who have become customers, and the same rule applies: If they cannot be uniquely identified using only their data, then they are not social consumers (or prospective customers) [see Figure 5.2].

Unlike the moment a social consumer becomes a customer and identifies themselves, for businesses no clear point exists where a prospect must self-identify during their decision-making process. Most often, companies require self-identification only at the point of purchase, or perhaps at the point of registering for a discount or coupon, when consumers have already made their decision. Therefore companies might have thousands of names in Excel spreadsheets, Customer Relationship Management (CRM) applications, or other data stores collected from Internet newsletter signup sheets, at trades shows, or other events, and not know anything other than an email address or, at most, prospects' names and locations.

It is unlikely that these sparse data points can be tied directly to one or more social profiles and therefore, they are not truly part of the company's social community. Recall that segregated enterprises remain rooted in the mind-set that consumers are pursuing a relationship with the company, while Big Social Mobile enterprises believe that the company must work to become part of the consumer's social circle—so that they can then leverage these relationships to reach additional prospects.

To analyze your universe of prospects, ask yourself the following questions:

- How many prospects has the company made contact with? When was each of these contacts made?
- How usable is the information gathered during these initial meetings via traditional methods your company has used in the past, such as direct email, email "batch & blast" techniques, phone, or in-person visits?
- How many of these prospect records contain bridging data and how many of these prospects can be connected to profiles on any social or mobile platforms?
- What is the total size of the company's social community on all social and mobile platforms? And, can this be determined down to the individual, so that these individuals can be categorized as prospects or customers and appropriately marketed to?
- How does the number of customers your organization has compare to the number of prospects it has gathered data on, what percentage has

bridging data, can be identified as social consumers, and can be identified across both the physical and digital landscape? What is the quality
of this information?

If a company has launched digital initiatives in the past, it is likely that it will
already have thousands of followers in its social community, all of whom are
clearly social consumers and can be leveraged. But segregated enterprises cannot automatically tell which of these social consumers are also customers,
which are prospects, and which are neither. Integrated enterprises, however,
understand and fine-tune this analysis. Customers who are only connected via
social media alone are less valuable than those who have also interacted with
the enterprise via web sites, emails, salespeople, and Customer Service; these
traditional interactions are tracked in Customer Service, CRM, or other enterprise applications, and when these interactions are combined with an analysis of social and mobile behaviors—contained within the big data collected by
the company—they offer far richer insight into the behavior and mind-set of
each individual consumer and groups of consumers the company is interacting with.

Organizations will need to break their digital prospects down into smaller,
more workable groups. First, they will need to note those prospects that are
uniquely identified in both the digital and physical world—whether their data
inside the traditional enterprise is connected to their social or mobile profile, or both. This group of prospects can then be segmented in many ways:
through the *explicit information* that they have provided, such as personal
demographics; through *implicit information*, such as their level of interest;
through information about them that can be *derived*, such as what product
they are interested in; through *social information*, such as who they are connected to or what their interests are; or through their *behavioral information*,
such as what sites, pages, or files they have visited and for how long. These
social consumers will also be segmented by how engaged they are with the
brand and their sentiment [see Figure 5.3].

Second, they will need to identify which prospects are identifiable only in the
data stores created by real-world interactions. Third, they will need to identify
those who interact on clearly identifiable digital sites, such as websites, social
platforms, or mobile applications. Fourth, they will need to identify those about

Types of Information

Explicit Information – information the consumer has specifically provided, such as their email address, phone number, name, date of birth or other information solicited through direct (although sometimes creative) methods.

Implicit Information – things that can be inferred about the consumer based upon other information (of different types) gathered, such as their propensity to buy or product of interest. Implicit information is often confirmed through the use of explicit methods.

Derived Information – what can be determined to be factual based upon other information provided, such as calculating age based upon date of birth or determining products of interest by combining explicit information with social and behavioral information to derive an appropriate list of products for a specific consumer.

Social Information – reveals the relationship between the consumer and other consumers, their interests, activities and hobbies, the locations at which these occur, and often the nature of their relationships, such as peer-to-peer or consumer-to-influencer.

Behavioral Information – the factual activities in which a consumer engages, such as the websites they visit, the terms they search, the links they click on, the position and duration of their mouse on the page or those activities which occur in the physical world, such as where they go, who they call or meet with and what stores they frequent.

Figure 5.3   The five types of information (or data) that integrated enterprises use to better understand consumers.

whom the organization has almost no knowledge except data points such as those contained on mailing lists.

Collectively, the consumers within these groups make up the entire target audience that the company currently has some connection to. However, from a data perspective, each of the consumers within these four prospect groups exists in a separate digital sphere. The goal of an integrated enterprise is to first identify and analyze their relationships with each of these groups of prospects, and then, over the long-term, connect these spheres so that any consumer interaction can be tracked across disparate spheres and also across both physical and digital landscapes. Only then can their benefit to the organization be maximized.

Use the following questions to categorize your prospects:

- How many prospects can be identified in each sphere? And, how many can be clearly identified across both the physical and digital landscapes?

- How many and which platforms are these identifiable prospects using? How does this compare to the platforms being used by the customer base?

- How many of these prospects, and which specific ones, became customers? Via what channel? Were any prospects converted to customers as a direct result of social or mobile interactions? If so, how many and which ones?

- Which of the five types of information—explicit, implicit, derived, social, and behavioral—can the company use to better analyze and understand its prospects?

SOCIAL INFLUENCERS

As important as it is to analyze the organization's relationship to digital customers and prospects, because they are the consumers that will directly generate revenue, organizations also need to broaden their analysis of their digital relationships to include those who can influence the organization's customers and prospects. I call these people *Social Influencers*.

Companies will already know some social influencers from their experience in the real world: financial analysts, leading members of the media that cover their industry, better-known journalists, columnists, and even online magazines and prominent bloggers. These can be easily identified, and they are usually willing to build a relationship with companies. These relationships may be formal, wherein the company pushes out controlled, marketing-oriented messages. They may also be adversarial—columnists or bloggers make a living providing information or insight that often contradicts the company's messaging. While all companies are aware of these influencers, Big Social Mobile enterprises seek to manage and leverage these relationships using a more inclusive and strategic approach.

Giant Eagle, a $9-billion food retailer that is one of the largest in the nation, takes a very aggressive approach to managing its relationships with social influencers. "We actually spend a lot of time and put a lot of resources to engaging our influencer network," says Donna Pahel, senior manager of interaction and online marketing. "So predominant bloggers in our geographical footprint, we are constantly educating them, holding events for them, and creating things where they can engage and incent their audiences and getting them to educate on our behalf and advocate on our behalf. We have found that those earned impressions are invaluable. When we do these events and we get those guys talking about us it is like friends and family talking it. It's not Giant Eagle telling you their own stuff is great."[1]

Giant Eagle is identifying and analyzing their relationship with social influencers throughout its community; the better it understands them, the easier it will be to figure out what it needs and how to reach out to them in a way that makes them friendlier to the brand. These influential people often will not join the company's community except to gather information; the company must join theirs in order to effectively engage them and, ideally, to leverage them.

To analyze relationships with social influencers, you should ask the following questions:

- Which public figures have the most influence on specific target markets that your company is seeking to penetrate? Which of these have the most dominant social presences?
- What platforms are these influencers using? What is the number of followers per platform, what does the overall mix of followers across these platforms look like, and how are they trending over time—which are gaining and losing influence?
- For each social or mobile platform, how many influencers are using it? Does the platform influence the tone of these influencers? Is their tone different from one platform to another?

* * *

Big Social Mobile enterprises also seek out "hidden" social influencers. These influencers are hidden because they have not yet reached a significant level of celebrity in the real or digital world. Nonetheless, they wield influence within a target market. These people can only be found when a company segments its markets into smaller groups. Within these smaller target markets the social circles are tighter because the community members more closely share demographics, interests, viewpoints, behaviors and even actual friendships or family relations. These smaller market segments adopt a form of groupthink—or more accurately, what I call *digital groupthink*. They experience the same desire for conformity and are therefore more likely to be less analytical in their decision making; they value loyalty and have difficulty expressing opinions or taking action that might alienate them from the group; but since their connection is digital they are more willing to express alternative opinions. As a result they are more susceptible to being influenced by these hidden social influencers.

Many organizations can identify these hidden influencers. Social subject-matter experts often have access to information or technology that rates the "klout" of individual social contributors. Those with a higher klout score are considered to be people whose opinions, comments, posts, and content reach more people and have greater impact. These hidden influencers, like their more recognizable counterparts, are creating content and going above and beyond to educate their audience, drawing connections that help people think differently about a subject, in addition to providing their insight and opinion. It is this value-added information that makes these influencers respected by the broader consumer base, and results in their higher klout scores.

However, while social media practitioners may have the ability to identify these influencers, they do not have the information or expertise necessary to connect with them at a deeper level. Within segregated enterprises this leaves the company exposed, since the influencer may not have accurate insight into why the company operates as it does, why it has created products or services in the manner that it has, or what future plans might be influencing its decision making. It also leaves these influencers open to build deeper relationships with the company's competition.

To overcome these challenges, integrated enterprises have their social media practitioners work directly with managers or other subject-matter experts, such as engineers, product developers, technical developers, trainers, or internal consultants, who have the detailed information and content necessary to deepen the relationship with and sway the opinion of these influencers—often having them interact directly. Only these experts have the ability to assist the influencers in increasing their influence, and, while doing so, can shape the influencers' opinions to the organization's best advantage.

Companies can identify these influencers by performing the following analysis:

- What are the major subsegments of the markets that the company is pursuing? How are these subsegments reflected in online communities?
- Who are the most influential people within these subsegments? Are they less-known media personalities or organizations? Who are the most active contributors that create the most engagement or get the biggest response when they post content to social communities?
- What platforms are these influencers using and on which are they most willing to engage with your brand? How many followers do they have per platform, what does the overall mix of followers across these platforms look like, and how are they trending over time—which ones are gaining and losing influence?
- How many influencers are using each social platform? Does the platform in use change the tone of these influencers? Which platform is best for your organization?

Once a company has identified the full spectrum of influencers, it can begin to understand its relationship to them in greater detail. The company should analyze these less-known influencers in the same manner as they did popular influencers, figuring out the viewpoint of each, where they stand in support or opposition to the brand, and how large their social circle is. This will reveal which ones are worth pursuing, and how they can be best used by the organization.

PARTNERS

The low cost of entry and operations on social media and mobile technology, and of the Internet in general, gives companies an opportunity to partner with organizations that in the brick-and-mortar world would be cost prohibitive. Integrated enterprises can create partnerships that expose their product and services to new markets, extend their brand's reach and influence, and create value-added content—generating more revenue than either company could alone.

This behavior can be seen through the proliferation of the group coupon (from which Groupon took its name) or deal-of-the-day industry. This industry has become a standard Internet model because it is a partnership between two companies that are both working together to create synergistic benefits. For little expense, both companies reach new markets, become part of previously untapped social communities, create new content in the form of news posts and coupons, and generate revenue that could not otherwise be created. The not-for-profit federation of motor clubs AAA, for instance, is boosting its performance by creating deal-of-the-day offerings. AAA has a passionate, active community of over 51 million members. By partnering with technology providers, it was able to leverage this community to create an entirely new division and revenue stream.

Analyzing the organization's relationships to digital partners, then, is an essential task for integrated enterprises—enterprises that prioritize connecting digital consumers to each other and the organization. Partnering has become a more significant organizational endeavor because in the new social economy, information can often be used as a form of currency. AAA could create a deal-of-the-day program not because it has a large community—there are many buying groups that would find it impossible to launch this type of initiative—but for three key reasons:

1. The combination of a large community and a technology infrastructure that makes this community available to partners (available in the form of usable big data)
2. The ability to analyze big data, providing insight into the preferences of its community at both the group and individual levels
3. A management team that values integration and understands the importance and power of digital initiatives despite the traditional beliefs and values of the automobile industry; they grasp the synergies that are possible when untraditional linkages are created

*   *   *

Consider these questions that can help you evaluate potential opportunities to partner:

• What new partner opportunities has the company entered into that rely upon its digital initiatives? What has the reach of these efforts been, and how much revenue or other tangible value have they created for the company?

- What digital assets does the company have that other companies might find valuable? This might be information stores, behavioral data, quantified expertise, or the datafication of new processes or procedures.
- What partners within your organization's supply chain can integrate their data into your company's enterprise data so that performance across an entire supply chain can be measured? How can this perspective be used to create efficiencies?
- What partners does it make sense to share customer-facing processes with (including processes that get customers to incrementally share information about themselves or that aid in their identification)?

Answering these questions can help organizations think about and work with digital partners in a much more holistic—and profitable—way. Approached this way, companies can use these partners to extend their reach. Because digital initiatives can easily take on the look and feel of different companies (as long as the core value proposition remains the same), they can be used to enter new geographic markets, new industry verticals, or market subsegments, or combine with new offers, such as with original equipment manufacturers (OEMs), without generating the high cost or creating the risk associated with new ventures. A company can combine its product or service with an expert in these areas that helps it create an entirely new value proposition.

COMPETITORS

Companies spend significantly less time researching their competition via social media, or analyzing the mobile applications of their competitors, than they should. Part of what people find so appealing about social media is that it is largely unfiltered. People say, share, or comment on whatever they want, often without restriction. This creates a goldmine of opportunity for companies to see what their competitors are doing behind the curtain, what they plan to do, and what they believe are their strengths and weaknesses. More importantly, it provides insight into what the market thinks of a company and its competitors relative to each other.

You can gain this insight by joining the social communities of your competitors, watching their news feeds, and even asking questions. If your competitors are using a segregated model—where its social media is managed by a social practitioner who may not understand exactly what should and should not be shared—you will find that they are willing to provide competitive information that was never before available: new or planned product and service offerings, new features and functions soon to be released, upcoming pricing and promotions, newly acquired customers or new opportunities they are pursuing, or even their financial position.

However, most organizations—everyone from the owner of a local small business to the social media analysts of a Fortune 500 brand—will find the effort of joining the multiple platforms your competitors are using (under an anonymous user name), monitoring their activity, and comparing it to your own organization's activity, engagement, and presence simply too cumbersome and time-consuming to be effective. But new, mobile technology is helping.

Perch, a mobile application created and distributed by Closely, Inc., helps companies focus on doing just that. By entering and selecting a competitor's company by name, the Perch application will collect information from all of their social feeds across many different platforms and bring it together so that it is easily reviewed and monitored (see Figure 5.4). At the same time, the application is gathering data about the competitor's activities and their resulting reach and engagement, and comparing it to your own company's performance. The result is a simplified workflow that allows a manager in any department of an integrated enterprise, to quickly and easily see and understand what their competitors are doing.

"Business owners and executives are overwhelmed with the complexity and pace in which consumers comment and interact about businesses and their products," says Perry Evans, CEO of Closely, Inc. "By delivering a personalized stream of content narrowed down to just what is important to that one company, about both themselves and their competitors, we deliver a clear signal through all of the noise. Delivering this as a mobile application allows us to notify users when things urgently deserve attention, and allows them to fit its usage into their natural downtimes, such as in line for coffee or between meetings."

While this application and approach may seem most applicable to a small business whose local area is heavily influenced by what their direct competitors

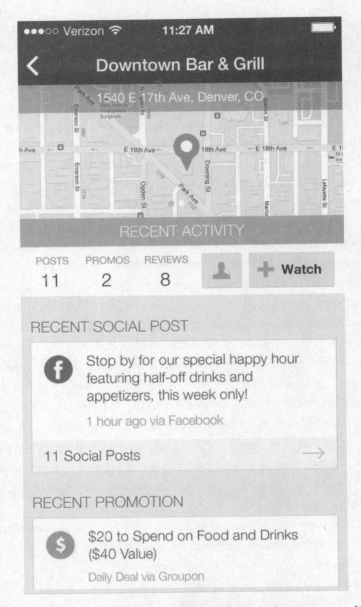

Figure 5.4 A screen shot of the Perch mobile application showing a consolidated social feed of competitor related activity.

are doing, consider that what influences many managers throughout even the largest organizations is also localized: the manager of a national chain restaurant location is still competing with other local restaurants, just as most sales people are competing within a geographic or industry segment against other sales people who are doing the same. Localized knowledge no longer means just a local town center.

You can also gain insight on your competitor's activity by becoming active within those communities that your competitors are not yet part of. Directly ask these communities about your competitors. Because your competitors aren't present and haven't yet established any positive sentiment, community members will be willing to tell you exactly what they think. This not only provides information about your competitor, but also provides insight into the groupthink of that community, revealing how it can be more effectively leveraged.

Analyze your competitors using these questions:

- Where are key competitors most present online?
- What do their social and mobile communities look like in comparison to yours?
- Do their posts and the engagement of their communities reveal whether they are using an integrated or segregated approach?
- What features or functionality are they using within these communities and applications to increase or influence interaction?
- What are they doing well, or poorly at, that your company should take into account or advantage of? The goal is not to duplicate their efforts, but to take the best part of them and make them your own.

MULTIPLE (ONLINE) PERSONALITIES

If an organization does not analyze their social and mobile communities to identify and understand these five types of digital relationships, they will not know who they're actually interacting with online or the complex but critical web of connections between them. Of equal concern is the fact that a consumer may have multiple personalities online; one or none of these multiple digital personalities may actually represent the real person or persons, or represent a customer or influencer without the company's knowledge. Any of these might also be a competitor. There are also small social communities sharing information or working in concert to understand a company's true position on a topic, the options that the consumer has or how they might maximize discounts. Companies often fail ro realize the implications of this complexity.

Many of the leading rental car companies offer a discount on their next rental if customers complete a survey after they rent a car. One rental car company failed to take into account how well connected highly mobile social consumers are and how consumers might have more than one role within a community. These customers figured out that if they used the coupon provided after the completing the survey, it negated other discount options available on check-out, thereby actually increasing the cost of their next rental. This information didn't make front-page news, but it spread through the social community—which is also the densest collection of the company's most valuable customers. The real loss for this rental car company wasn't the incremental revenue lost by underhanded (even if inadvertent) couponing; it was the loss of loyalty their social consumers felt, and the damage done within the company's social circle, because the company failed to understand that a customer or a prospect might also be a social consumer, and might also be influential—or even a competitor

Companies literally do not know who they are dealing with anymore. Integrated enterprises overcome this by actively working to identify individual consumers—to have them self-identify, to verify them, and to proactively identify them where they can't or won't. This helps them not only leverage consumers more effectively and appeal to them in the more consistent and helpful manner that the social consumer prefers, but also helps them avoid mistakes and reduce risks. But analyzing digital relationships in and of itself adds no extra value to a company. It is what you can get them to do when you understand them that is most valuable. And the key to doing that is understanding how you are currently interacting with them—as we will see in the next chapter.

Chapter 6

DEFINING CUSTOMER AND CONSUMER INTERACTIONS

NOW THAT YOU ARE AWARE OF the five types of digital relationships your organization has formed, you should look at each of these relationships from a pragmatic, historical perspective. More specifically, you should understand each interaction that your organization has had with each consumer—from the moment you first interacted with them until the moment the consumer stops being engaged with your organization. Doing this will establish a baseline that shows the relationship between the results that these interactions are creating versus the ideal results, or behaviors, that you are striving to produce

This analysis may reveal that some consumers behave in ways that are far from ideal. Prospects will fail to become customers, customers will depart too quickly, influencers will fail to influence in your organization's favor, and competitors will counteract your intentions. These discoveries, though, provide information that allows your organization to become more effective and move toward the Big Social Mobile ideal.

This analysis will apply most directly to customers and prospects, and to a lesser extent, influencers. You may find that with some influencers your organization has had no interactions; you have not yet built a relationship to be leveraged. In these cases you should try to determine who they have been interacting with and the impact this has had on your decision making. For partner organizations, examine their interactions comparatively—how their interactions compare to your own and how a partnership might make both of you more effective. It is likely that you have had no interaction with competitors, but the techniques discussed in this chapter will help you analyze how well (or how poorly) they're leveraging their digital relationships.

To provide a sense of the value that can be derived by defining customer interactions, consider this example of an organization that benefited from this knowledge.

KNOWLEDGE FUELS PERFORMANCE

National Oil and Gas, marketers of Marathon, Phillips 66, Sunoco, and Clark gasoline and diesel fuels as well as co-located convenience stores, was having problems with their customers who traveled on highways or interstates through their service areas but often didn't know about their stations. Customers would randomly choose a station, selecting the one closest to the exit ramp or choose the one with the lowest advertised gas prices. Those customers that did select National Oil stations often failed to fill up their tank completely, didn't always shop in their convenience stores, and sometimes failed to come away feeling any loyalty to their brands—all behaviors that were in the company's best interest.

While National Oil was aware of these customer behaviors, they did not have a holistic solution that would change them; they also lacked an understanding of how they might capitalize on specific behavioral changes. They decided to partner with iSign, a provider of wi-fi and Bluetooth mobile technology that delivers location-aware messages to consumers, engaging them at both the right time and the right place to influence behavior. iSign's technology uses a physical device to communicate with mobile technologies that enter its area, gathering data from these devices, and sending back to them, via text message, an offer. While this offer could be anything depending upon the needs of the company, National Oil offered potential customers a $.10 off per gallon of gas coupon when they filled up.

The theory was that potential customers driving down the local highway would pass the iSign antenna, receive a text message, and know that the cheapest option to fill their tanks was the National Oil station just ahead. The company recognized that text messages have the highest and quickest open rate of any communication method. Of the over 2.7 million connections made, over

15 percent of viewers not only read the National Oil text, but clicked through to accept the coupon. It changed consumer behavior and resulted in over 8,000 additional gallons of fuel sold at the station's pumps.

This is the power of mobile technology. But it still isn't Big Social Mobile behavior.

This approach only overcame the first problem: finding a National Oil station and choosing it over the competition. It made National Oil a more profitable gas station. But it didn't overcome other problems: ensuring that the consumer filled their tank, propelling customers from the pump into the convenience store, and creating loyalty among this new customer base. Overcoming these problems represented significantly greater value and improvement to the bottom line for the company. But to clear these hurdles, National Oil had to adopt a fully integrated approach. They had to go beyond customer behavior to the behavior of consumers in general; they had to bring two different internal departments—fuel and convenience stores—together into one strategy, and they had to understand and measure success in a way that went beyond selling gas or convenience items—they had to sell both. They also had to analyze what worked across multiple channels, incorporating consumer behavior, environmental factors, and financial transactions, blending big data and traditional data.

National Oil set out to change consumer behavior—to get them into their convenience stores. They required that the coupon be redeemed at the register. This meant that some consumers might not redeem the coupon, passing the station by entirely, but from the company perspective this forced customers to behave in a way that was most profitable. The profit on a gallon of gas is insignificant compared to the average margin on convenience store products. And once consumers were in the store, they could be targeted by additional marketing and coupons.

National Oil's strategy resulted in significantly greater in-store traffic, greater sales basket value, and more credit card transactions processed. In addition, 54 percent of the customers that used the coupon also joined the company loyalty program. And this was only the beginning. The company could also perform analysis on the data generated and tie sales to local temperatures, weather patterns, and customer demographics to determine what coupon price and offering would have the biggest impact by time of day, day of week, user device, and other variables.

iSign technology differs from typical mobile location-based technology that requires what is called "geo-fencing," large longitude and latitude defined areas. When customers approach the coffee kiosk or even when they pass it by, the technology is capable of targeting them with an additional coupon—this time for coffee and a donut. The data revealed that 74 percent of the time that teenagers can smell food, the coupon motivates them to buy. Big data, social, and mobile technology all were working together to improve National Oil's bottom-line results. [See figure 6.1]

National Oil would not have achieved these results if it had failed to understand how prospects could be converted to customers and how customers can

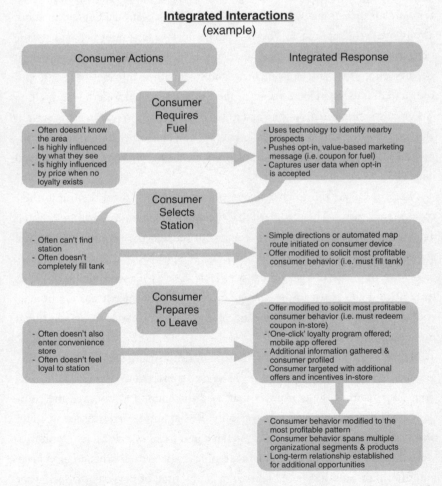

Figure 6.1 How an integrated enterprise maximizes each interaction with consumers to elicit the most beneficial behaviors.

be upsold and cross-sold to drive tangible business results. The company gained this understanding and leveraged it by focusing on how its digital relationships responded to specific interactions; it analyzed where it was successful getting customers to behave in ways that were most profitable to reveal how it could elicit these same behaviors from other customers and prospects.

In most organizations, each department or division operates independently, and each focuses on customer behavior specific to its own area. The management team in charge of one channel does not concern itself with how other channels operate or how they appeal to prospects, customers, influencers, and partners. The tactics, and sometimes even the strategy, used by one area of the business is rarely adopted or even considered by another. Getting consumers from the fuel pumps into the stores is something everyone understands to be in the organization's best interest, but is not something anyone is actually responsible for. Conceptually, it is simple; in practice it is highly complex.

To get past this complexity, organizations need to understand how they are interacting with consumers and connect these interactions to the appropriate people, processes, and technology within the organization. National Oil was successful, in part, because it took an honest look at how it was interacting with customers and consumers—even if the interactions weren't ideal.

Understanding how your organization is interacting with consumers with respect to each of the five different types of digital relationships is a step that can't be skipped. Focusing on just prospects and customers and connecting their interactions with different people and processes within your organization will be tremendously beneficial, as National Oil discovered. But by analyzing all five groups, the organization will be in an even better position to determine what overarching behavioral patterns produce the most significant benefits.

To many organizations, this seems like a daunting effort. They often doubt their ability to follow customers as they interact with consumers in the real world—the foundation of being "customer-centric"—let alone also following consumers across the digital landscape. Integrated enterprises, however, recognize that despite the additional effort, if they are unable to follow consumers through the numerous transitions they will make from the physical to the digital and back again, they are unable to provide them with a consistent experience, reshaping their behavior regardless of landscape or medium. The integrated approach allows them to understand what interactions help and hinder consumers from behaving in ideal ways and allows them to redesign entire customer-facing processes or specific interactions to achieve better results.

National Oil accepted that adopting an integrated approach would be challenging and would require them to take a fresh look at how they interacted with their customers and consumers. But it is this effort that allowed them to see behaviors that would improve tangible results within one sales channel—increasing revenue from fuel sales—and dynamically improve their results across multiple channels and mediums—increasing high-margin product sales within convenience stores in addition to the increased fuel sales and improved long-term loyalty. None of this would have happened had they not learned how to better define their organization's interactions with consumers.

TURNING CUSTOMER-CENTRIC INTO CONSUMER-CENTRIC

To become customer-centric is challenging. It requires the ability to see and understand each interaction from the customer's perspective. While challenging, when organizations adopt this perspective, they can connect customer behaviors to the people, processes, technology, and information within their company that have the biggest impact upon the customer's experience, so that they can then improve that experience.

In the past, few companies were willing to redefine internal processes to best meet customer expectations. Certainly there were already companies that built their entire business model around this goal—such as Nordstrom's, the best retail shopping experience on the planet; Apple, the best consumer goods technologies; Disney, the best entertainment experience—but for the average company, average service levels had long sufficed. But this attitude has changed over time—the movement to become customer-centric is now widespread.

But the leap from customer-centric to *consumer*-centric is one most companies have yet to make. It is a significantly greater challenge.

A big part of what makes this leap so challenging is that organizations cannot clearly define what a consumer is. The definition of a consumer can vary wildly from one department to another, one channel to another, or even from one executive to another. It is often highly influenced by which specific types of consumers, customers, prospects, or influencers each individual employee actually interacts with. Leaders therefore often struggle to understand how they can get their organization to present one consistent impression and experience to consumers when they cannot even agree upon a consistent definition. At the same time, leaders understand that because digital mediums allow consumers to interact with them at any time and place (and often without consumers identifying themselves), digital initiatives have forced them to be concerned about the consistency of their organization's interactions with consumers across different mediums, segments, channels, and even individual employees.

In the face of this challenge some leaders panic. I've witnessed management teams become paralyzed by the need to change from a customer-centric to a consumer-centric model. When this happens, they convince themselves that they must revolutionize the entire organization or reinvent themselves—a sure path to fulfilling the eight-year rule. In so doing, they end up eliminating their most viable essence in favor of something that lacks inherent or intrinsic value.

Instead of attempting to reinvent themselves, organizations should do something that feels counterintuitive to becoming consumer-centric: *Begin with a very narrow definition of customer.*

This is the process that Seattle City Light, a municipal power utility, used when they won the *Business Finance Magazine* Vision Award for their progressive use of performance management techniques contained within *The Performance Power Grid* (Giannetto/Zecca, Wiley, 2006) to become customer-centric. They began the process by defining exactly when a consumer became a customer: typically signing a contract, making a purchase, or placing an order. From there these customers were categorized according to their primary needs. As a power utility (attempting to become customer-centric), this meant grouping them according to residential, small business, large projects, and new construction. From this initial moment, each customer segment was then tracked through its own process until they become happy, satisfied customers. Along the way each customer segment touched a wide variety of people, processes, and technology; a wide variety of information was required to understand this path. Some segments, such as residential and small business shared resources—Customer Service. And sometimes they didn't share resources they actually should—Engineering. But the process was laid out exactly as the customer experienced it.

Seattle City Light discovered gaps between what they expected their interactions to be and reality. For instance, management assumed that power was turned on for a customer on the date it was requested but learned they sometimes failed to collect information about exactly when the customer wanted power. They also found that sometimes their customers lacked access to essential information about their services that they had assumed customers could easily find. This revealed to management what the customer experience was and how it needed to change.

Defining customers in this narrow manner may seem like a simple process, but it is often challenging. Consider a typical power utility. These organizations tend to see themselves as generators and deliverers of power, as engineers, as people who work in crisis-prone environments. Given this traditional perspective, the customer is almost an after-thought, and the consumer is non-existent; power utilities concentrate on the operational side of their business. And those who deal most directly with customers—Customer Service—are often the lowest-paid employees with the highest turnover rate and the oldest technology. Some executives don't have any idea what it takes to turn a consumer into a customer, let alone make them happy.

Given this background, it should come as no surprise that organizations struggle to follow the path of a customer through their organization, to see the obstacles that the customer encounters, and even to see the obstacles that their own employees face when they attempt to help these customers with their problems. Customer interactions fade into the bureaucratic background while operational emergencies, financial issues, and other matters take precedence.

Despite all the talk in organizations about customers, the reality is something quite different, especially when it comes to defining customer experiences and behaviors, and responding to them. Have you ever attempted to get Legal, Finance, or even HR to do something counter to standard processes and industry norms because it is in the customer's best interest (and the company's long-term best interest) and met stiff resistance? Have you ever encountered the pricing conflict between Sales, which wants the highest margin to improve their personal compensation, and Operations, which often wants to focus on customer adoption to drive long-term marginal contribution? This is a reflection of organizations' inability to see things from any other perspective but their own.

Understanding your own organization as the customer experiences it is eye-opening; concentrating on a narrow definition of what a customer is makes this process easier. As we will see, this is just the starting point—later this effort can be expanded to include all consumers, and then further refined for each customer segment and even subsegment. In the end, this analysis can and should be conducted from many different customer perspectives (customers in different subsegments, with different demographics or even different attitudes and opinions, inherently see the same interaction differently). These many perspectives can be winnowed down by answering these questions:

- What are all of the interactions that your organization has with consumers that actually turn them into customers, both digital and physical (typically moments within financial transactions)? Which of these produce the most customers, the most revenue, and if possible, the highest margin?

- For each group of consumers who became customers via the same interaction, define the people, processes, information, and technologies—all of the additional interactions—that they then must interact with before they become happy, satisfied customers? This should include any major documentation, both physical and digital, web forms, phone calls, demonstrations, meetings etc. that are necessary.

- For each major process the customer encounters, what are the major requirements to make the process possible (for example, a customer order is required before a product can be pulled from a warehouse or staff assigned) and the necessary outcomes, such as a sales orders, products shipped, or staff creating deliverables?

- When a customer becomes dissatisfied, or requires additional goods or services, what are all of the interactions along the paths they take to make these additional purchases, have their problem solved, or stop being a customer? What missed opportunities exist along these paths where the company can retain customers about to depart or maximize the value of those who are willing to make additional purchases?

EXAMINING CONSUMER INTERACTIONS

As important as it is to focus on how customers are interacting with your organization, it can't stop there if your organization is to create one consistent impression and experience for all consumers—if it is to become consumer-centric. In a new social economy, prospects, influencers, and partners—sometimes even competitors—represent tremendous value when they can be leveraged, value that far exceeds the revenue and profit they produce. Therefore, the same analysis that allowed the organization to understand how it is interacting with customers must be expanded to include consumers in general.

Companies have traditionally defined how they wish to interact with consumers by first defining their market channels: direct or indirect sales, wholesale versus retail versus ecommerce, or partner channels. Each of these sales channels uses specific sales techniques that allow for the greatest exposure of their brand to these groups: retail locations, trade shows, and websites or third-party ecommerce portals. Localized marketing and sales processes and materials are then created to support each of these channels.

Some companies define how they would like to interact with consumers by first segmenting consumers based upon consumer needs. For a power utility, the needs of a residential consumer are inherently different from the needs of a commercial location or a multiyear construction project. These obvious customer groupings define the marketing and sales processes that will support them. These approaches reflect how the company believes it will be the most effective and efficient at attracting customers from different customer groupings. As a result the company creates different impressions of who they are, and the experience consumers have when interacting with them will vary.

Customer-centric companies use a different approach. They segment the market based upon their understanding of the consumer. Starbucks, for example, essentially offers one product: a high-end, sophisticated coffee-oriented experience. As the chain expanded outside Seattle, they first targeted areas based upon consumer demographics such as average income, real-estate values, age, and percentage of disposable income. These demographics defined their primary markets and where their first new stores should be located. Their secondary markets were areas that had positive scores in many of these demographics but not all. Stores in these areas could be proportionately scaled down in cost but still had to maintain the same overall look and feel if the customers were to have a consistent impression and experience. This approach worked with great effectiveness since they were in essence bringing something of value to the consumer's community. It was a value-based transaction. The company gave them an experience they could not otherwise get and consumers gave them revenue. Because the experience was consistently positive, customers also became loyal. The company understood these consumers and how they could get them to exhibit the ideal behaviors they desired by adopting sales and marketing processes and techniques that reinforced, or more specifically solicited, behaviors that were in the company's best interest.

Starbucks succeeded because they clearly defined who they were and supported this with one consistent experience across their entire organization. They could have handled it differently, especially in the face of failure. Once Starbucks saturated their primary and secondary markets, they moved into tertiary markets—groups of customers who share some of the same demographics but not enough to create the same "ideal behaviors," as we will label them in the next chapter. Within these areas, their standard marketing and sales approach and the consistent look, feel, and experience of their retail locations could not create the same ideal behaviors that generated the revenue or loyalty required to make stores in these areas sustainable over time—eventually leading to their massive store closures of 2008.

It might therefore seem impossible to become truly consumer-centric; the market is too big and diverse.

Starbucks' massive success—new store openings and growth rate equaled by few other companies in history and none ever within their industry, the evolution of the US coffee consumer to new levels of sophistication, the redefinition of what American coffee is—and its failure—massive store closing, rapid withdrawal from numerous markets, allowing McDonalds and fast food brands to steal large market share—reveals how a company can actually become consumer-centric; how it can succeed and what will cause failure.

What is different about the consumer-centric approach is that it must start with only one thing: what makes your organization valuable to consumers. And from this one thing springs the answer to how the organization must approach the market: consistently. Whereas the traditional approach is to create multiple sales channels and then create processes, design marketing materials, and hire sales people that will be most effective in those channels, the consumer-centric approach starts by defining what the company brings to market—a world-class coffee experience, the best entertainment experience, the best consumer good products, or even affordable but reliable products. From this one starting point, a consistent message and experience can be built.

Starbucks, Dunkin' Donuts, 7-11, the corner kiosk, and even the traveling coffee truck are all competing for the same consumer dollar, but doing it in different ways. However, while a sophisticated coffee drinker can still afford a cup of coffee at the corner kiosk, someone who only has $1 simply cannot buy a $4 cup of coffee—not every day. Starbucks cannot be all things to all people, just as all people cannot be convinced that a McDonald's latte might actually taste better; personal opinions about the brand might preclude it. This is what caused nearly uniform failure in tertiary markets for Starbucks. They could not incentivize these customers to behave in ideal ways, or more specifically they *could* (for example, they could offer steep discounts) but it would not be sustainable. Starbucks' failure was not being able to detect and understand the behaviors of these consumers until it was too late, until they had already fully invested in these markets.

The same technique used to understand customer interactions can also be applied to consumers in general. Using a clear statement of what your organization stands for and the value your organization will add to the consumer's life as a starting point, you can then ask how consumers will react to it. In turn, you can break consumers down into meaningful segments based upon their different demographics and situations and their differing views on needs versus value. Different consumer segments will respond differently; some will respond positively, and others, no matter what the company does (as Starbucks learned), will respond negatively. You can then begin to structure how you will interact with each segment through a step-by-step process that eventually leads consumers to become customers.

To understand the interactions that your organization has with consumers, answer these questions:

- How do customers first become exposed to the brand and in what ways do they investigate it?
- How do they understand and validate its offering?
- How do they express their needs or show interest in the products or services?
- Do they refer to other people (influencers) or resources during their decision-making process? How do they interact with these influencers?
- When do they get serious about making a buying decision and what triggers this? And when they do, how do they narrow down their choices and what drives them?
- What price, promotions, features, or functions do they investigate or inquire about the most before they make their decision?

Analyzing this process reveals the intricate web that shows the relationship between potential customers and the organization, and those other, external entities that also influence the decision-making process—external entities whose opinion customers rely upon during the decision-making process. This is the process of prospects interacting with influencers, deciding among competitors, buying from the company or through partners, and finally becoming customers—this behavior seen and understood through the eyes of the consumer. Although digital initiatives have made this process more complicated, they haven't changed the logic of this decision-making process itself. They have only added more options and information. The process of connecting behavior to the enterprise remains the same despite the new mediums that connect the physical and digital landscapes.

Beginning with the value proposition also has another, highly beneficial effect: through it, the company is creating one consistent identity within the market. It is not pretending to be high-touch in one channel and a low cost provider in another—not unless this can be clearly explained and consistently understood by the consumer. It is firmly grounded upon those things that have made it successful, and more likely to avoid losing sight of its true value—more likely to adopt an evolutionary than revolutionary mind-set. Since digital initiatives, especially social media, are accessible to every consumer regardless of what category they fall within, this approach allows an organization to have one voice in the market that speaks for all of its channels. And this highly unified, consistent message is what the social consumers expect and demand, and what opens the door for their long-term, more passionate connection to the brand.

DIGITAL CONNECTIONS TO THE ENTERPRISE

When you define the interactions that customers and consumers have with your organization, the tendency will be to define the interactions that occur in the physical world, or through traditional channels. This is natural. These are the interactions that are a result of processes that have been in place throughout the organization for some time. As a result, most of these interactions will leave a mark—they will appear as a digital fingerprint that details a customer order, a request for more information, a website visit, an email being sent, or any of the other numerous interactions that might occur. But others, such as a sales person using a phone to call a customer or a retail sales associate answering a random question while passing a consumer in an aisle, may be undetectable because no record of these interactions exists.

Big Social Mobile enterprises actively seek to ensure that even these interactions are captured. They cultivate information about every interaction, recording, monitoring, and analyzing it as if it were the basic substance from which money is made—and it is, at least in terms of gaining insight into how behavior is translated into tangible value.

When defining each interaction and reviewing the information available relative to it, you will discover that two things are occurring. First, some interactions are designed to leave a fingerprint but don't—or at least fail to do so some of the time. Therefore, in cases where data about these interactions should be available but is sporadic or incomplete, you can focus on improving the internal process that creates this information. For example, sales people often call customers but fail to record that they did. If this action is not recorded digitally it cannot be used to determine (for instance) how many and which touch points are necessary to convert a consumer to a customer. The process of recording such calls must be enforced or made easier.

Second, some interactions have no process in place to record their occurrence. How can a retail sales associate record a random question from a passer-by consumer? It is notoriously difficult but can be done. In many retail locations these sales associates now carry tablets. When consumers approach them they answer their random question but also attempt to engage the consumer in further conversation. To make this conversation meaningful they ask for personal information: a loyalty number, phone number, email, or other identifying information. During this exchange, the sales associates uses the tablet application to record the interaction. Other companies solicit this information at checkout by asking if the customer received help from any associate or if they have been in the store looking for this product during prior visits. While these checkout counter methods do not define interactions with the accuracy that integrated enterprises desire, they provide them with a starting point from which to improve.

Using a mobile device to document an interaction that would previously have gone unrecorded is now standard practice in integrated enterprises. Social and mobile technologies not only allow organizations to interact with consumers and customers within their communities, they also generate, store and share data about these interactions. These technologies are most often the starting point for creating the five types of data: explicit, implicit, derived, social, and behavioral. This data reveals to companies more information about consumers than they would otherwise ever be able to solicit from consumers on their own. Therefore, this information directly fills in many of the gaps that exist when consumers interact with the organization.

For example, when a customer makes a purchase at a retail store there are several levels of data made available to the retailer, the distributor who provided the product to that retailer, and the manufacturer who made it. The availability and sharability of this information can be generalized at three levels:

- If a customer is part of a loyalty program then all personal (explicit) information about the consumer is available to the retailer, and may also be available to the distributor and manufacturer if the retailer has chosen to partner with these organizations to make it available to them. Since loyalty programs are typically attached to social media—through a social login—then the consumer's social information and some of their behavioral and implicit information are also available to these companies. Since the consumer has made a purchase, he or she is uniquely identified. If this identification is attached to the customer's actual profile, then all of the implicit and behavioral information is available. From this, these companies can any derive information that can be calculated or inferred.

- If a customer has made the purchase using any credit device most (but not all, largely depending on their level of sophistication, terms, conditions, and relationship with the credit provider) retailers will then know explicit information about the consumer. This information is often not passed to distributors and manufacturers in detail, but may be passed in summary form. For example, the retailer's partners will know the quantity of products or services ordered and may know the demographics of the purchasers, but will not know them individually. If retailers can connect this customer to any information in any of their enterprise, social, mobile, or big data stores—via bridging data—they will know everything about this customer.

- If a customer pays cash and leaves no personal digital fingerprint during the interaction—they do not provide their phone number or email address, participate in a survey, utilize a rebate or coupon, later register the product online or provide any other bridging data—then they are not uniquely identifiable. In this case, the retailer, and its partners, will only have detailed (explicit) information about the transaction and not the customer. Anything that can be derived from it is possible, but it typically cannot be attributed to one individual person.

*   *   *

Today, digital interactions provide organizations with nearly all of the information they need to understand how they are interacting with consumers, and the resulting behaviors.

In addition, any interaction conducted via social or mobile—or through a site with social login, or that collects bridging data, or that uniquely identifies a consumer behind the scenes—supplies similarly useful information. Any action a user takes on nearly any website is also recorded—everything from the click path, the hovering behavior of mouse pointers, the time spent on each page, the information downloaded, even sometimes forms only partially filled out. Smart phones, tablets, laptops, computers, and increasingly even televisions, cable boxes, gaming consoles, any smart device (anything from light bulbs to automobiles) connected to a consumer's personal device via an application or the Internet also supply a range of information that adds greater detail about how consumers and customers interact with organizations and their products.

When taken in total, this information—digital fingerprints from interactions across both the physical and digital landscape, the correlated information from social and mobile technology, the big data from smart technology—clearly defines how the organization is interacting with the outside world. For integrated enterprises this information is invaluable; it provides them the leverage they need to influence consumers and outpace their competition. And it can be used in many ways, ways that makes the organization generate more revenue or profit, or operate more effectively and efficiently. It can also be used to understand how well the current interactions of customers and consumers conform to the ideal behaviors that are most beneficial to the organization—the focus of the next step in becoming a Big Social Mobile enterprise.

Chapter 7

IDENTIFYING IDEAL DIGITAL BEHAVIORS

NOW THAT YOU'VE DEFINED HOW YOUR organization interacts with consumers and customers (or any of the five types of relationships), it is important to compare and contrast these interactions with their ideal behaviors—those behaviors that lead to the best outcome for your organization. It may be something simple: Perhaps consumers who view online video content are more likely to purchase your products or services than those who never do, for example. Or it could be something more significant: Those consumers who actively engage the brand across both the digital and physical landscape generate greater revenue per transaction and have greater customer lifetime value than those who only engage online, for example. The process or pattern of interactions your organization uses must solicit or elicit these ideal behaviors.

Let's look at two organizations that identified ideal digital behaviors in different but highly effective, integrated ways. Then, we'll look at how to apply the lessons from these examples to your organization.

In the beginning it didn't look as if Netflix's new video by-mail rental service would be sustainable. After the initial surge that came with the newness of its by-mail offering passed, Netflix began suffering the same problem common to the retail-based movie rental industry: Customers didn't rent often enough to make the business profitable. The company had a subscription-based model, with a recurrent charge, and customers would quickly drop their contracts, leaving Netflix to carry the revenue loss that came from acquiring them as new customers in the first place. Netflix could reduce marketing expenses or the amount they paid their partner companies for each new subscriber, but both of these reduced their market presence and would quickly kill the company. Lacking any physical presence that made them part of the consumer's community, they had to find some way to make their service more present in their customers' lives; they had to change the way consumers thought about them, and how they behaved.

The first solution that began tipping the scales in their favor was the creation of functionality that on the surface seemed minor: allowing users to create a queue of movies that they wanted to watch instead of asking them to order movies one-by-one. Netflix could then continue to send new movies as soon as they received the old ones back. This not only made Netflix more present in their customers' lives, it made it more likely that customers would increase the number of movies per month they had in rotation. Both of these strategies helped get their customers behaving in ways that were more beneficial to the company and helped make the Netflix business model sustainable—increasing average customer retention to 25 months and Customer Lifetime Value to an average $291.25.[1]

Wireless carriers Verizon and AT&T were up against a similar problem. Customer turnover in the industry averaged 1.8 percent of customers per month. This number was troublingly high, especially considering the need to offer steep discounts that in some cases caused a net loss on new client equipment purchases at the start of their contract. But these discounts were common practice since analysis proved that the number one reason for customer turnover was the average age of a device—customers were most susceptible to switching carriers when needing a new phone. If a customer did not stay with one carrier for a significant period of time, that carrier could not earn back its initial loss—Customer Lifetime Value heavily influenced their strategy.

However, one carrier in the industry challenged the common view. They segmented their customer base by profitability per customer. They found that among their most profitable group of customers, the primary behavior that heralded their likelihood of switching carriers was a drop in average monthly recurring charges. When these customers reviewed their contract to reduce their average monthly fees—for whatever reason they decided to do so—they were most likely to switch carriers. Among this group of customers, the average

age of their equipment was only 20 percent as strong an indicator as average monthly customer value was—implying that a short-term view was necessary.

The solution was a significant change for this carrier. They would have to base their long-term strategy on Customer Lifetime Value, but their tactical approach on monthly revenue per customer and behavioral triggers. Their Customer Service Agents, retail associates, Internet websites, mobile applications and partner network—all of which interacted with these customers at critical moments—would have to adopt new processes that incentivized their most profitable customers to stay at exactly the right moment, when they were most likely to switch. Only this combination of customer behavior and company response could maximize customer value.[2]

The changes this telecommunications company was facing were significant. But they had identified something valuable: an ideal customer behavior that would directly result in tangible business value. They had done it by analyzing customer interactions—the data that reflected them—to uncover this ideal behavior, or more accurately, a behavior or moment in time at which the customer or consumer could be manipulated to elicit an ideal behavior. In this case, this ideal behavior was the continued loyalty of their most profitable customer segment. In an industry where margins are low and competition is high, this type of discovery could be the difference between surviving and dying.

In any industry, identifying the outcomes that are in the best interest of the company is valuable. But it is at the heart of what makes Big Social Mobile enterprises more effective than their segregated competitors; it is what makes the costs associated with integrating digital initiatives into the enterprise worth it; it creates the tangible business results that executives are seeking.

As important as it is to understand your company's digital relationships and how you are interacting with them, it is only when these five types of digital relationships begin behaving in ways that benefit your organization that additional value can be created. Therefore, the next step in the process of becoming Big Social Mobile requires your organization to identify those behaviors that are most beneficial to them. With this knowledge, you can create more valuable interactions.

Companies often fail to identify ideal behaviors and fall short of the Big Social Mobile ideal because they define success for these digital initiatives based upon standard, subject-matter-defined objectives, such as increasing followers, engagement, sentiment, downloads, or data processed. Digital initiatives are then never required to measure their success in ways that align them with core functions of the business: increasing revenue and profit, decreasing expenses, improving operational effectiveness or efficiency, or other things that directly drive these results.

There is also a tendency to use project milestones—creating a presence on each social platform or launching a mobile application and then launching each successive new release—as the measure of how successful these initiatives are. When these initiatives are implemented using a segregated approach, the milestones never include objectives such as identifying consumers, prospects, and influencers, creating a digital linkage between physical customers and social consumers, and removing the multiple online identities that consumers often create.

Ideal behaviors fall into two different categories. The first are those that are specific to a company's strategy—long-term loyalty versus maximizing shopping cart value or minimizing transaction cycle-time versus accepting a longer sales cycle in order to create greater intimacy. The second category comprises those behaviors that are ideal because if consumers do not behave in a specific way, the organization cannot operate as an integrated enterprise. Integrated enterprises require information in order to take back power in the corporate-consumer relationship, appeal to social consumers, leverage relationships, and measure success and failure. Therefore, they constantly seek to acquire information that allows them to more effectively interact with specific consumers. This means that within every segment of every social community, the most important of these types second types of behaviors is to get each consumer to first tell you who they are.

THE ART OF SELF-IDENTIFICATION

Companies have long understood the value of knowing exactly who their customer is. The photography consumer goods company previously mentioned issues over $20 million worth of retail rebates, but their primary objective was not to improve sales but to capture consumer information. They knew this information was valuable—not only did it provide them insight into consumer behavior that influenced their strategic approach, it also allowed them to improve sales incrementally by micro-marketing.

Investing this type of money to collect consumer information was standard practice for years. Before the proliferation of social media it was actually relatively easy for companies to identify their customers. All that they had to do was offer them something of value, typically a discount. This easily evolved into loyalty programs; many readers still carry small, plastic barcode IDs on their keychain. This standard practice was quickly integrated into ecommerce platforms: customers had to create profiles if they wanted to register for discounts on a website or order a product. In all of these cases, the consumer told the company who they were—they self-identified.

Social media has made the identification of consumers more difficult because interactions are no longer transactional in nature; they are conversational. Companies can't ask consumers to fill out web forms before they can talk to someone from the company; this was acceptable ten years ago, but now consumers will not tolerate it.

Social platforms targeting consumer adoption reinforce this mind-set. They do not require consumers to self-identify. Most consumers do choose to self-identify, because it is often in their best interest to do so, such as on professionally oriented social platforms, or because building a network on any legitimate platform relies upon people using their real names and supplying information about themselves to connect with people they know. But companies cannot actually rely upon this data, or more accurately, they cannot create processes and a data management plan based upon it. Today's social consumers are smart enough to understand that companies are trying to identify them and will often go to extreme lengths to prevent it. It is not unusual for social consumers to have a separate email address that they use when interacting with companies that they are unsure they want to build a long-term relationship with.

But consumers will tell a company who they are if they believe the relationship will be valuable to them. As a result, organizations must be ready and waiting when a consumer is willing to tell them who they are in exchange for something they believe will be valuable. In segregated organizations, this readiness is unlikely, since only the social media practitioners are focused on interacting with consumers through the platforms they manage. These experts aren't concerned with a person's true identity—if you ask many of them if they know who these people actually are, the question will visibly startle them. Integrated enterprises focus on getting consumers to self-identify; they then verify this identity and have widespread awareness of and responsiveness to consumer online behaviors. They are attuned to the path that a consumer takes—from that first moment they have the tiniest inkling of a need that the company might be able to satisfy to the moment they become a customer, and beyond.

The moment consumers self-identify is of vital importance because creating consistent interactions across Marketing, Sales, Operations, and Customer Service interactions, through any medium, with social consumers, is not possible without uniquely identifying who they are. In addition, personalized interactions are not only more effective at converting social consumers to customers and improving customer loyalty, they are also more effective at using customers to extend the reach of the enterprise, expose them to new markets, serve as influencers, and achieve other benefits.

Here are the points on the path (in reverse order) where consumers often self-identify, given certain conditions:

- When they become an actual customer, if the process is not overly cumbersome; and when becoming a customer is tied to additional benefits, such as warranties, use-case information, discounts on accessories, etc.
- After the consumer has made a decision to purchase from your company but before the actual purchase, if there is an incentive. While it seems as though this might be unnecessary (since they have already made the purchasing decision), remember that your competitors will be willing to offer their highest discounts to steal them away at exactly this same moment
- During their deepest research on the limited number of final options they have selected, if they have access to information that will help them more than the general information available to them
- At any time during the research phase at which a mobile application appeals to them
- At the onset of their research if the overall brand appeals to them on a personal level and is able to emotionally engage them

These moments will vary by company, industry, and business model, as will the way in which a company motivates the consumer to self-identify. But what all of these points on the path have in common is that they attempt to offer something of value to the consumer in order to get them to behave in a way that is in the company's best interest. And it is important to note that the consumer is not making this decision based upon *actual* value; the consumer is making this decision upom *perceived* value. The consumer is exchanging their personal information for something they *perceive* will be of value to them. The use of perceived value can trick them into doing it—as we saw with the rental car company issuing fake coupons—at the risk of sacrificing brand loyalty and alienating social consumers.

Answering these questions will help you understand whether your company is taking an integrated approach to consumer self-identification:

- What different points in your marketing and sales processes allow or cause customers to self-identify? Which of these points are most effective at getting them to do so? Do you measure this conversion?
- What incentives are being used to get customers to self-identify at these critical moments? Are they truly valuable to the consumer or are there other things that consumers would find more valuable?
- How certain are you that your digital consumers are supplying you with reliable information? When comparing data from different digital spheres, does the same phone number or email address (or other key data points such as name combined with address) appear for different people?

*   *   *

The art of getting consumers to self-identify is quickly becoming a science, thanks to mobile technology. Mobile devices are unique and typically used by only by one person. These devices allow only a single instance of an application to be installed on them. Although multiple people might log in to that application, the app itself will manage who is who and pass this information back as part of the (big) data stream it generates. The company tapping into that stream will be able to differentiate users. This means that a phone number (and often an email address) is one of the few data points that allow companies to bridge the physical and digital landscapes for individual consumers. This is part of the reason companies run SMS campaigns, often tying them to television or radio advertisements. When a consumer responds, not only does it allow the company to know who in the market is considering a purchase, it does it in a way that uniquely identifies them.

This is a behavior of Big Social Mobile enterprises. They use one medium integrated into another so that behind-the-scenes data from one sphere is integrated into another. This allows them to consistently engage the consumer regardless of where that consumer is on the physical or digital landscape. When a consumer responds to a television advertisement using their phone, they are actually beginning a digital conversation with the company. This will generate a series of strategically placed advertisements on the Internet while this consumer is browsing, accompanied by emails and perhaps even hard mailings sent to their home. Eventually, if the company's campaign is effective the consumer will make a purchase, call them on a phone and tell them who they are or even appear before them in a retail location—probably with their smart phone in hand to verify everything that the salesperson says is accurate.

The ability of a company to follow a consumer across both the digital and physical landscape seamlessly is only possible when the company has fully integrated these digital initiatives into their enterprise and into each other, and significantly easier if they have convinced the consumer that it is in their best interest to self-identify.

GETTING CONSUMERS TO SHARE

What happens when a consumer won't tell you who they are? Companies must be adept at getting consumers to do digitally what they have been doing in the physical world for decades. They must invent ways to interact with consumers so that they can slowly get to know them. Eventually they will be able to uncover enough information about a consumer that they will be able to identify them and then use the right triggers to turn them into customers. Without the ability to uniquely identify consumers, companies cannot craft personal, highly-tailored sales and marketing messages that are significantly more effective with social consumers than generalized techniques.

Although the complexity of today's physical and digital environments is creating an exponentially more complex relationship with consumers, the technology itself facilitates consumer identification. Within each digital sphere technology is working hard to help companies get to know their consumers. Some technologies operate behind the scenes (consumers are unaware that they've been launched by an interaction) and look for unique information about the user that has been stored on their device when they visit a company's website. Other technologies place a small bit of information on the user's device that becomes an identifier; some devices have a unique address of their own; others record the unique address of the location a device is connecting to the Internet from. These unique numbers then become the person's "name," tracking their behavior until their true identity can be determined. This method allows companies to monitor individual behavior within specific digital spheres: visiting websites, reading or downloading information, using mobile applications.

Technology today is capable of all of these things. However, in a segregated enterprise the emphasis is often not put on using technology to actively identify consumers because those in charge of the initiatives are not tasked to do so. They are tasked with achieving initiative-specific objectives. Integrated enterprises ensure that their websites, social platforms, mobile apps, and the processes that support them are all working to achieve this objective when they are designed.

Integrated enterprises use these techniques to build a record of who they are interacting with and their demographics, what their common behaviors are, what their social community looks like, and what their interests are. Even without knowing exactly who they are, companies can still understand consumer behavior and personalize their targeting and content. Let's say a consumer is considering adopting a cat. Suddenly their browser will be full of advertisements for cat furniture, toys, and food; video sites begin suggesting cat videos. Once the system can detect the person's email address, it will soon identify emails and email advertisements featuring cat-related products. This is the most basic technique marketing technology uses behind the scenes to help companies better target consumers using the information they have learned about them.

This is marketing targeted to that consumer, but it is not highly personalized because the company or companies working together have not uniquely identified the consumer. They will continue to pound away at the consumer with incentives, tricks, and behind-the-scenes techniques in hopes that they can. At some point the consumer will begin to receive these cat-related advertisements across all of their devices because they have been identified across multiple digital spheres—even if companies still don't know exactly who the consumer is. And until they do they will collect one small piece of the consumer's identity after another until they can complete the puzzle. When the puzzle is finally complete they will attach all of this retained history to the person's true identity, completing the picture of who they are, the opportunity they represent, and the interactions, or pattern of interactions, they will respond most effectively to.

Companies rely on multiple techniques to facilitate self-identification, including:

- Regularly searching consumer devices for personal information
- Placing unique identifiers on consumer devices (often called cookies) that can then be tracked by the company
- Identifying the unique location from which the device is connecting to the Internet
- Using incremental surveys that ask the consumer for one or more small pieces of information each time they visit a location within a network
- Asking for unique "bridging data" each time the consumer actively interacts with them through any sphere
- Employing gamification techniques that use competitive behaviors to motivate consumers to disclose information
- Offering incentives—sometimes you just have to pay them to get them to share

Within segregated organizations, these techniques are only marginally effective. While these companies can have personal and meaningful interactions with individual consumers through any one medium—conversations on social platforms, SMS exchanges via mobile, chat sessions on the Internet, or phone calls to Sales or Customer Service—they cannot follow an individual as that consumer moves from one medium to another, from the physical to the digital and back again. They cannot provide this individual with a consistent, highly personalized experience that actively moves the consumer toward the moment of conversion. More specifically, they cannot guide each consumer toward the interactions or patterns of interactions that are most likely to get the consumer to behave in an ideal way.

To achieve this goal, social and mobile data must be connected to enterprise data so that the information contained within this big data can be used to create a uniform customer or consumer experience across multiple channels and mediums, and shape their behavior as necessary. Disparate digital initiatives must be integrated with each other and into the enterprise. This allows the company to know specifically who an individual consumer is, calculate the current or expected value of them as a customer or consumer, identify where they stand in the decision-making process, and perhaps even learn what will motivate them.

Fortunately, social and mobile platform providers now understand how important it is to companies that consumers share information about themselves and are making it easier to collect this information. Since these platform providers are themselves being forced to create fully integrated, profit-driven usages of their technology, they are creating functionality within their platforms that tracks a consumer across different locations on the digital landscape and in some cases the physical world.

For most companies, social logins begin this function. These logins allow consumers to use their core social profile, typically on one of the major providers, such as Facebook, Google+, Twitter, or LinkedIn, to log in to less well known websites or to link their profile from one platform to another. Social logins work anywhere across the digital landscape, bringing together multiple social platforms, mobile applications, and traditional websites (see Figure 7.1).

Janrain, the first company to make social login possible using an existing ID from any of the major social platforms, quickly realized that despite how much consumers liked social logins (consumers are more than 50 percent more likely

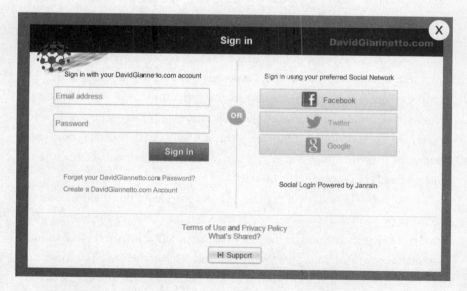

Figure 7.1   The social login on DavidGiannetto.com powered by Janrain technology.

to register for a website if it has a social login[3]), the real value of their technology was using the data they were collecting to create a richer, more meaningful relationship between their clients and their clients' digital customers. Over time, what began as a simple approach to unify consumer usernames and passwords quickly became a customer profile management platform.

This technology provides the information that becomes the foundation of integrated enterprises. It not only gets consumers to share their identity, it connects them across multiple digital spheres—social and mobile platforms, and desktop, laptop, and mobile devices. For companies this means that the power of what was once an isolated community on their stand-alone website becomes multiplied, because social login not only increases membership, it provides more information about that consumer's behaviors, social circle, demographics, interests, posts, and other information. Information that the consumer would never give to an individual entity becomes available and is used to uncover the profitable patterns and segments discussed in the next chapter.

Social login also provides an organization with the "bridging data" necessary to connect big data to traditional enterprise data at its lowest level: the individual consumers. This allows an integrated enterprise to create a consistent customer experience across multiple mediums and channels. Traditional departments—Marketing, Sales and Operations—are seeing the same identity and information about a consumer when they interact with them as those within the organization's digital initiatives.

"This is allowing organizations to think differently about customer information," says Larry Drebes, CEO of Janrain. "Where once they relied solely upon sales transactions and customer relationship management updates to understand the consumer they were talking to, they can now look at who that actual person is—their likes and dislikes, their behaviors, and their social circle—and treat them like individuals. This means that not only can they create consistent marketing messages from one interaction to the next, they can have consistent and personal conversation one-on-one."

Social logins also allow organizations to consolidate the multiple online digital personalities a consumer might have, remove false identities, and more frequently identify consumers the first time they interact with them—all things that make integrated enterprises more efficient. This added insight into who a consumer is means that an organization can understand the full extent of the consumer's social network, and their importance within it, so that they can use it to extend their reach and influence.

To assess your company's ability to incentivize consumers to share information, answer the following questions:

- After analyzing the traditional enterprise data relative to your customers and consumers, are consumer identities identifiable across multiple platforms? If you perform this same analysis on datasets relative to the digital spheres your company operates within, what are the results?
- Are the major social platforms that your company operates on also connected to the communities you store and analyze data from? For example, do you use social logins, and do customers log into a website to register or request information?
- What physical and digital processes does your company have in place to learn more about customers and consumers incrementally? When you audit these processes, how effective are they?
- When your company offers broad discounts, coupons or rebates, what information are they getting in return for these offers? Does your company focus on growing and using information as a company asset?

Despite the insight they provide, the real power of social logins comes from their consumer adoption rate. For consumers, these logins provide real value; they don't have to remember as many usernames and passwords or fill out one profile after another. Consumers are willing to try a new social community or website because the effort to gain access has been drastically reduced. Social logins get consumers to share—to behave in an ideal way—because the consumer sees value in them: it makes their life easier.

BEHAVIORS THAT CREATE REAL VALUE

For many organizations, their social community is managed separately from the core functions of their business that generate real, tangible value—processes that facilitate and fulfill financial transactions. To become an actual customer,

When mapping out the consumer's journey from initial interest to final conversion (during which they will self-identify or share enough information to be identified), organizational leaders must think outside of the box that their experience, business model, or industry might force them into.

Club 4Sixty6 in New Jersey decided to break down the barrier between their social community and their customer community. If you visit their Facebook page or their company website, you will see an abundance of social tie-ins, including Facebook and Twitter social logins—common to many sites. But while their websites will allow users to get a feel for whether or not this is a club they'd like to frequent, their events, DJs, and services (including several full-service restaurants), visitors are frequently prompted to use the social login before they can see pictures or videos or other detailed information.

It would be easy to assume that this is because Club 4Sixty6 is building a community that it can effectively market to—and it is. But it doesn't end there. Club 4Sixty6 uses a technology called TidalWave on its web sites. What TidalWave does is break down the barrier between social and customer communities by allowing for a financial transaction to occur directly within the social platform. In technical terms, it reduces the number of interactions the company must have with the consumer as the consumer is converted to a customer (or when viewed from a customer perspective: the number of actions a consumer must perform to become a customer). But TidalWave is doing much more—it is adapting the consumer's behaviors to the company's ideal behaviors.

While nightclubs are looking to make sure they have enough people in their club to make an event or evening profitable, what they are really trying to do over the long-term is create a community of upscale clients who are willing to upgrade their services: buying the more expensive bottle service, booking private lounge areas, or combining a dinner experience with a nightclub experience. These customers not only generate more revenue per transaction (event) for the club, they also bring in more people of a similar nature. Club 4Sixty6 is using a technology to exhibit these behaviors from this community by first making it easier for people to behave in these ways, and then creating greater community among this group and *their* social communities. This mimics and reinforces the behavior of these small social communities when they are in the club itself—sharing the private areas and expensive drinks—and also makes it easier for these people to share the great experiences they had at 4Sixty6 with their community—multiplying the club's reach.

This is social, mobile, and even big data working to create ideal behaviors.

TidalWave also does something else that allows Club 4Sixty6 to operate as an integrated enterprise, bringing these digital initiatives together with their operations in the physical world. Book a bottle service through Facebook, or even leave a fingerprint that shows you are considering one, and TidalWave will execute a workflow that results in a salesperson—or an event coordinator—contacting the consumer to make sure they are going to have the best experience possible. As community members register to attend the event, providing demographic information about their club-related preferences, the technology alerts the group in charge of ordering supplies so they have the right amount, alerts the entertainment staff on the average musical preferences of attendees, prompts marketing to make decisions to increase or decrease promotions, and alerts management to update financial projections. All areas of the organization are using data-driven information to maximize the profitability of the event. This is Big Social Mobile behavior and relies upon these digital initiatives being integrated throughout the enterprise—getting consumers to behave in ways that are ideal and the enterprise reacting in ways that are in the best interest of their social community, but also themselves.

This is why companies seek to identify and understand consumers: so that they can sell to them and then sell more to them. While experts and support personnel within the enterprise may lose sight of this fact, executives cannot. Only three ways exist for an organization to grow: create new customers, sell more to existing customers, or increase prices. Sooner or later, every company must adopt one or a combination of these three as their strategy. All portions of the enterprise must be equally focused upon its achievement—even digital initiatives.

When the enterprise fails to focus on this goal, initiatives don't produce tangible business results and executives become frustrated—a reasonable reaction given how much time and money their companies have invested in these initiatives. Integration, therefore, is the solution. Full integration can be seen within Club 4Sixty6: Product Management creating an event; Marketing advertising it and measuring market response; Sales selling it and gaining feedback on what works and what doesn't; Operations working hand-in-hand with customers. At each step along the way, each group is feeding back to the groups that precede them how the product or service itself is perceived; how it is marketed or sold; and how it is delivered and needs to be changed for better conversion rates or increased customer sales. This is how a company forces its products and services, along with the processes that bring them to market, to evolve, gain traction, and produce tangible benefits for the organization.

This fully integrated, value-producing approach runs counter to the conventional wisdom and so-called best practices for social and mobile initiatives. Typically, social and mobile subject-matter experts focus on increasing engagement with the consumer base, in conjunction with promotional or discounted offerings that will prompt consumers to buy. This approach is equivalent to a *push* marketing campaign delivered via newer technology: it is an attempt to reach as many people as possible via as many mediums as possible so that even a small success rate will create additional revenue. At best, this strategy yields modest results. Increasingly, however, consumers aren't responding to it at all. What they are now responding to are more personalized approaches—the antithesis of push techniques.

Integrated enterprises are doing all of these things to identify the behaviors that are most likely to convert:

- A consumer to a customer
- At the lowest cost for the highest prices
- Most quickly
- In a way that places the new customer in the position most likely to buy additional products and services—generating the highest customer lifetime value possible

* * *

To assess your organization's ability to understand what consumer behaviors create real value, answer these questions:

- How effectively are the core processes of your organization working together to reiteratively improve your conversion rate? Has the conversion rate been improving over time?
- What new product or services, processes, or techniques have been introduced based upon these improvements and how have they improved the conversion rate of the organization?
- How do the processes that create customer conversion vary across the physical and digital landscape? Have equal resources and organizational

focus been applied to improve them, and as a result, which are more effective? Can the best parts of each be leveraged to create a best-practice approach internally?

- What is the value of each customer market segment at its lowest granularity? Which is the most valuable in the short-term and long-term?

- Are these groups defined by traditional methods: products purchased, channels to market, geographic locations, length of relationship? And, can this same analysis be done based upon the five different types of data: explicit, implicit, derived, social, behavioral?

- Can your organization show, in clear, specific terms, the patterns that lead to the highest conversion rate, the highest revenue per transaction, and other positive outcomes discussed throughout this chapter?

PREFERED BEHAVIORS FOR EACH CONSUMER SEGEMENT

Not all digital consumers are alike, and therefore to determine what behaviors you're seeking, you need to break these consumers into the five distinct groups we identified earlier: customers, prospects, influencers, partners and competitors. Your first goal is to encourage them to self-identify, and if that doesn't work, then you must discover a consumer's identity on your own. Analyzing behavioral patterns for each group is crucial, since when you understand each current pattern you possess the key to generating additional revenue; you can steer each group toward those behaviors that will create greater revenue directly or indirectly; you can identify the groups within your organization that are or should be interacting with consumers at these critical moments and shape processes that solicit them.

By segment, here are some of the behaviors that Big Social Mobile enterprises should strive to create within their digital relationships.

CUSTOMERS

As previously discussed, ideal customer behaviors are those that lead them to purchase products or services, to purchase more of these, and to be willing to purchase them at a higher price. Other specialized metrics such as community growth and engagement are helpful, but they don't necessarily drive purchasing behaviors, no matter how engaged they might be; or even if they do make purchases, revenue from them isn't maximized just because they're engaged members of the community.

Analyze the pattern of interactions for those that maximize both short and long-term rates of return, so that you know which behavioral patterns produce the highest revenue per transaction (or preferably margin per transaction) and which produce the highest customer lifetime value (again, marginal contribution is preferred). The two patterns will not be the same. But you can use the differences between these patterns to shape your approach to the market, choosing a strategy that positions the organization properly.

In addition, integrated enterprises place a higher value on customers who behave like social consumers. These consumers are likely to act as influencers, connecting with other consumers and providing them with information or recommendations that turn them into customers. Segregated organizations focus exclusively on turning consumers into customers, while integrated enterprises take a more sophisticated approach, seeking to convert social consumers to customers but also converting traditional customers into social consumers.

Beyond these behavioral goals, here are other behaviors that integrated enterprises seek to generate among their customers:

- Share any information relative to *why* they did what they did. Did the videos posted provide them with information that was specific enough to prompt a purchase, was it the personal phone call or email from a sales person, or was it the way a sales associate was open and informed about the consumer's other options? While companies often use the insight gained from big data to infer these reasons, there is no true casual relationship between data and behavior. The only way to know for sure is to ask.

- Provide a qualitative measure of the company's performance that helps the company improve the effectiveness or efficiencies of its processes. Companies possess overwhelming amounts of quantitative data, but qualitative data about organizational performance is much more difficult to come by. Digital customers are often more willing than the other four groups to supply this type of information.

- Offer suggestions for product and services, features and functions, processes and technology improvements for the organization; get them to function as an extension of the enterprise in their desire to see it operate more effectively and efficiently.

- Define the organization's place within the competitive landscape, and provide information relative to competitors' products or services so that it can compete more effectively.
- Regularly supply additional detailed information about themselves and their behavior so that a company's understanding of its customer base continues to evolve. Data gathering does not end at the point of conversion (as it sometimes does in segregated enterprises).
- Reveal which influencers they find most influential, and why.
- Reveal the full extent of their social circle.
- Behave as influencers.

PROSPECTS

Just as integrated enterprises understand that connecting the physical and digital profiles of a customer will give them more opportunity to leverage and generate revenue from each customer, they understand that this is most easily done at the first point of contact—or rather, the first point of contact at which the prospect can be uniquely identified. Therefore, your primary behavioral goal for prospects is to motivate them to provide as much information about themselves as possible during the initial encounters.

Beyond this primary focus, seek to create the following prospect behaviors:

- Provide information into the products and services, features, and functions that they are most interested in, and what specific attributes they find to be most valuable.
- Reveal what discounts, rebates, or incentives, or what combination of products and services, would most influence them to become customers.
- Disclose what information, use case scenarios, or additional offerings would most incentivize them to become customers.
- Provide insight into which specific interactions they found valuable, and which added to or detracted from their willingness to interact with the company
- Define what variables they find to be most influential during their decision-making process, so that the company can use this information with them and other consumer groups.
- Share information and insight into what and who most influences them before they become customers.

- Reveal the full extent of their social network. This is done not only so that the company can market to this group, but also to find their connection to current customers or influencers with which the company has a good relationship, leveraging these connections to convert them.
- Provide this information relative to the company's key competitors, so that the organization is gaining insight into the actions it needs to take to achieve competitive advantage.

INFLUENCERS

You may remember the uproar Facebook caused when placing ads in consumers' social feeds that used a friend's picture to endorse a product—even though that person never agreed to be used in this manner. Facebook quickly ended this practice. But this approach did work, even though a majority of people didn't like it. It worked because these recommendations didn't feel as if they came from a company telling consumers how good their own products and services were; it was an impersonal third-party endorsement.

This first failed attempt to manipulate consumer opinion created a breakthrough; it showed the power of social influencers over consumer behavior, and actually proved that less well known or hidden influencers—those who were only influential within a given individual's own personal social circle—possessed just as much klout as well-known media figures and other well-known authorities. Consumers value opinions expressed via social media because they believe these opinions are objective (unlike messages conveyed through traditional marketing techniques). Therefore, you possess a clear objective when it comes to influencer behavior: Get them to endorse your products and services. Even if it isn't the unequivocal endorsement that the company might hope for, it is still powerful and certainly more beneficial than any criticism.

Influencers are also great resources for competitive information. Beyond serving as endorsers and resources, companies should strive to create the following influencer behaviors:

- Define what behaviors, characteristics, processes or other variables would make them view your organization most favorably. Influencers will often give you the answers to what will make them positively endorse your company and its products if they are actually asked.

- Define their peer group, who they are influenced by and why, and in their opinion what would make this group view your organization most favorably. Once a personal relationship with influencers is created, especially if it transitions from the digital to the real world, they are often willing to provide all of the details the company needs to more effectively interact with this group.
- Reveal what will make them view the organization, not just its products or services, favorably. This will not only create greater influence with the specific influencer, but will also be reflected in their willingness and enthusiasm to positively endorse your organization.
- Provide insight into where your organization stands versus your competitors—not just relative to their willingness to positively endorse your products, services and organization, but also in the opinion of the consumers over which they have influence.
- Reveal what makes them most engaged with your organization and what interactions, products, services, or organizational characteristics led to their engagement in general and at specific moments (for example their very first interaction).
- Define the level of interaction they are seeking.

PARTNERS

Integrated enterprises recognize that partners can take on a wide range of roles that benefit their organization. Partners can become extensions of the company itself, add extra value to existing products or services, serve as influencers, differentiate the company from competitors, and even help the company's business model evolve to the next best configuration. Motivating partners to take on these and other behaviors is sometimes more challenging than creating the behaviors associated with the previous three consumer groups (partners have looser connections to organizations than customers, prospects, and influencers), but the effort is worth it. Therefore, Big Social Mobile enterprises strive to have their partners engage in the following partner behaviors:

- Expose the organization to the greatest number of social consumers, consumers that are uniquely identified, and consumer groups that are identified as being most valuable.

- Share the processes that they are using to identify consumers, convert them to customers, up-sell, or cross-sell them or to prevent attrition. How do these compare to your organization's interactions?
- Share how they are collecting and using information, and share this information about their communities in a way that easily integrates with your organization's information.

COMPETITORS

Leaders should know where their competitors stand on the scale between integration and segregation. This will allow them to gauge the competitive threat they are facing, since becoming Big Social Mobile is a concept that all organizations will eventually embrace. Social, mobile, and big data subject-matter experts are extremely adept at performing this competitive analysis. While they may not fully understand the nuances of a competitor's positioning, they do possess the skills necessary to analyze competitive feeds, applications, and technologies to assess where and to what extent these digital initiatives have become embedded into these other organizations. They will also perceive how competitors are using these initiatives to add value to their own enterprise.

While organizations cannot force their competitors to behave in ways that most benefit them, they can analyze the interactions they are having with their communities so that these behaviors can be adopted, or at least countered. The following questions should be asked about competitive behavior:

- What interactions are they having with their community, via which platforms, and how do these interactions appear to be influencing their engagement and sentiment? Segment your competitors into two groups: traditional versus progressive. How does behavior differ among these two groups?
- Which actions are generating the highest engagement and the most positive sentiment for your competitors?
- Do interactions posted on social feeds reference any interactions that occurred through other mediums? This will reveal which internal company processes, if any, are integrated into their digital initiatives and in what fashion.

- Which of the ideal behaviors identified for each of the groups within this chapter are reflected on each competitor's feeds? What content are they providing that is soliciting these behaviors?

*   *   *

Beyond this analysis, it is routine for companies to monitor the social feeds of their competitors and the overall quantity and tone of media attention they are getting, just as closely as their own. This allows them to quickly exploit weaknesses and prey opportunistically upon trends.

Chapter 8

ANALYZING PROFITABLE PATTERNS AND SEGMENTS

ONCE YOU UNDERSTAND YOUR DIGITAL RELATIONSHIP to different types of consumers, how you are interacting with them, and how you would prefer to interact with them, you're prepared to segment and analyze your community, uncovering profitable patterns and segments your organization can capitalize on. These can be discovered through a variety of techniques that incorporate behaviors, trends, demographics, and other factors that help your organization understand which consumers are conforming to the ideal behaviors. This analysis can help you to identify how you can get those falling short of the ideal to behave in more profitable ways.

Let's look at one organization that used this step in the process with great success.

Comedy Central competes with a wide variety of entertainment outlets for the attention of its core demographic—males aged 18–34. This demographic falls within a sweet spot: old enough for alcohol and car advertisements to resonate but too young for the major networks to really begin competing for advertising dollars. For Comedy Central that is their "one thing"—the core value proposition upon which everything else is built, from the comics they select to their presence on multiple social and mobile platforms. And they've done such a good job at focusing on it that after 20 years in business they've saturated nearly the entire comedy market.[1]

How then can the network continue to grow? New television shows that go mainstream and draw massive new segments of audiences are hard to come by, and expensive. It's much easier to lure in new viewers by reusing content that will turn them into loyal network viewers that follow shows, storylines, comics, and anticipate the next comedy special or DVD that they could buy. But it is challenging to grab the attention of this demographic, all of whom are social consumers. The solution is to find times—however small—when their perpetually on-the-go target audience is available to be engaged; when they are looking for something to entertain them and relieve the boredom.

According to an analysis of behavioral data, males aged 18–34 are often bored on holidays—when they are stuck at "mandatory" events. During these moments they always have their mobile devices, and have already adopted the behavior of being more engaged with their phones than with their family.

Comedy Central capitalized on these small windows by pushing content out via social, mobile, web, and email channels with greater frequency during these times. They could analyze response to see what was working, and refine the process with each new holiday—each new moment when their audience was most available, even if each window of availability was very small.

Any organization can undertake this step of uncovering profitable patterns and segments if they understand how their organization interacts with each consumer segment and subsegment versus their ideal behaviors. With an integrated approach, the organization will be able to create a moment where this interactivity adds up to tangible value—in this case a nonviewer becomes a viewer (increasing advertising potential and multiplying the organization's reach) and a potentially loyal viewer (creating long-term value and again multiplying organizational reach). To accomplish this, the organization must have the ability to do two things. First, it must segment their communities at critical moments. And second, it must analyze their community and subsegments of it, to reveal with whom, when, and how they are most successfully getting consumers to behave in ideal ways.

These two abilities combine to create a feedback loop allowing the organization to uncover profitable patterns and segments. It can also spot consumers who are not exhibiting ideal behaviors, discontinuing those interactions that are having a negative impact and testing new interactions and patterns of interaction to create a closer-to-ideal response.

While all five types of digital relationships should be analyzed using this perspective, it is most applicable to customers, prospects, and influencers. For this reason, I'll focus on these three groups, alluding to partners and competitors as appropriate.

IDENTIFYING CRITICAL MOMENTS

An organization can segment its social community at any moment in time—following any interaction. If this were done at the lowest level it would separate consumers into two simple segments: those who did or did not take any given action. These segments might be meaningful for very specific analysis. For example, if a company closes its largest deal ever, it might be meaningful to look at every single interaction that led up to this deal in order to understand what led to that high-yield transaction (hoping to replicate it). Or, if a company wants to know how expensive video content impacts their conversation rate versus other, cheaper alternatives, that too might be analyzed in this way. However, a much more meaningful way to segment the business involves focusing on those moments that have the greatest overall impact on the organization's ability to create and retain customers.

Using these critical moments as starting points for analysis forces organizations to first focus on those actions that produce tangible value. It helps companies identify what *must* be done well if the organization is to have long-term success and avoid analysis-paralysis. Focusing on these moments also facilitates integration. By concentrating on a very specific action at a specific moment in time, it's much easier to involve multiple internal processes and departments interacting across both the physical and digital landscape. If an organization were to attempt a much broader analysis, leaders would feel (rightly) overwhelmed, struggle to succeed, and likely revert to a segregated mind-set.

Starting with these moments also helps the organization see that the approach to becoming Big Social Mobile is not fundamentally different from how organizations have traditionally segmented and analyzed their business, and also how they have measured their performance. Traditionally, companies segmented interactions with consumers at the moment of contact, again when they were qualified, again when they were issued pricing (in some models), and then at the moment of conversion. They measured success based upon the organization's or the sales person's ability to close opportunities or convert consumers to customers, either individually (as with high-touch sales) or in groups (as in retail environments).

Digital relationships are segmented in a similar manner, at those same critical moments. The difference, though, is that because social consumers will be leveraged and approached digitally, segmentation must include other moments, such as when they self-identify, download a mobile application or otherwise become uniquely identifiable.

Here are the seven critical moments when organizations should initially segment and analyze their customers and prospects [see Figure 8.1]:

- **The moment of initial contact**: when the organization first encounters a consumer it has never before connected with. Companies can break this group into subsegments by channel, platform, event, or other source through which they were encountered, by the product or service they are explicitly interested in, and whether they are truly a new consumer that has never before been encountered or might simply be a duplication of previously known consumers.

- **The moment they choose to self-identify**: when consumers choose to uniquely identify themselves to the company on any social or mobile platform or through any traditional process or interaction that stores their personal information. This group can be segmented by the sources through which they've self-identified or the explicit reason or interest that caused them to self-identify.

- **The moment the organization uniquely identifies them**: when a combination of interactions within one or multiple platforms allows for the unique identification of a consumer. Enterprises can then divide this group into subsegments based upon the sources through which they were identified.

- **The moment they are converted from prospect to customer**: when the first, initial financial transaction occurs between the organization and a customer. Companies should subsegment this group by the product or service purchased.

- **The moment they are cross-sold**: when a customer is sold a product or service in a different category than the one that initially caused them to become a customer. Companies should subsegment this group by the additional product or service purchased.

- **The moment they are upsold**: when the customer purchases additional products or services from the organization or its partners that could not otherwise be used by the customer without having made the original purchase. Subsegment them by their additional purchases.
- **The moment they depart from the organization**: when a customer declares they will no longer pay for recurrent goods or services, or after the average lifespan of the goods or services has been exceeded without the customer making an additional purchase. This moment may also include a pattern of nonresponses that shows that a consumer is highly unlikely to make another purchase. Segment these departing customers based upon the length of time or number of purchases made, the channel or products/services previously purchased, or the explicit reasons for their exit.

Companies can also segment and analyze other key interactions, such as when a consumer downloads a mobile application, follows the organization on social media, when their customer record is linked to their social profiles, or at those moments that have traditionally been important to the organization's

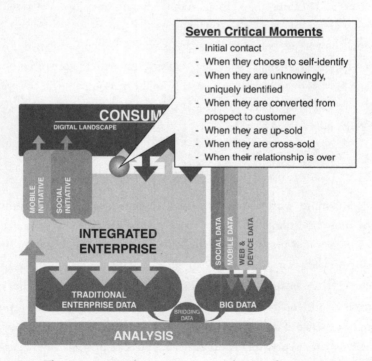

Figure 8.1 The seven critical moments most often used to segment consumer interactions.

business model. But the bulleted moments above are of primary importance. They form the foundation of how a company leverages its prospects, customers, even its influencers, and perhaps its partners.

This segmentation process will facilitate the integration of digital initiatives into the enterprise. None of the seven segments listed above include purely social or mobile consumers, just as none of the information analyzed is drawn purely from big data. The insights gained from this segmentation and analysis aren't only applicable to social and mobile practitioners. In fact, those who manage traditional business functions such as Marketing, Sales, and Operations and their supporters will benefit the most. Marketing will begin to use social and mobile, and the information contained within big data, to cost-effectively test multiple marketing messages (something too expensive to be done via traditional methods) to improve responses based upon consumer feedback; Sales will begin to understand that social and mobile are channels that generate new sales leads; Operations will use these digital initiatives to gain insight into which customers are dissatisfied, to improve their processes, and to adopt new methodologies.

Segment your prospects and customers, and to the extent possible your influencers and partners, into groups at the moments identified. Analyze these groups to determine consumer interactions that led to or away from ideal behaviors. As you get better at this analysis you will uncover other nontraditional subsegments that, at each stage of interacting with the organization, are behaving in ways that produce or detract from the best outcome for the organization. These new segments are created using a variety of techniques described in the remainder of this chapter.

TRADITIONAL FINANCIAL ANALYSIS

The most common form of analysis used to segment a group of customers, and the most traditional, is a strict financial analysis of the cost to acquire each new customer and the value that each customer adds to the business, either in the short or long term. Digital initiatives, especially those newly introduced to the business, are often divorced from these financial measures because it is difficult to calculate and understand their impact on revenue, margin or expense at the individual level. Such initiatives are often managed, especially when a segregated approach is adopted, as projects where expense budgets are assigned and revenue budgets are quietly absent. At the same time, subject-matter experts within these initiatives do not think in these cost-benefit terms, and the advice they receive from industry experts does not address or reflect this bottom-line mentality. A lack of financial accountability for digital initiatives is pervasive.

Because of this, it is not unusual to see a mobile initiative where it costs $4.00 to acquire each new customer, but the average revenue generated per customer is only half that amount, or a social initiative where the cost to acquire is four times the customer lifetime value. These initiatives are financially unsustainable.

A segregated mind-set, however, rationalizes the lack of financial accountability. It posits that big data, social media, and mobile technology efforts are "different" and that they deserve an exemption from the financial rigor under which all other corporate efforts are conducted. The segregated perspective isolates the success or failure of these initiatives and reduces their strategic value.

In reality, these initiatives can potentially contribute in many areas of the business: they get consumers to respond to marketing programs, create new leads for Sales, process customer inquiries and solve customer problems, resolve accounting issues on client accounts, or generate new employee applicants for HR—if they are integrated into the enterprise. An integrated approach to measuring the financial impact of digital initiatives, therefore, ensures that these initiatives will be implemented and measured based upon the outcome achieved. It is akin to treating digital initiatives as channels for each traditional function of the enterprise.

Start by relying on traditional financial analysis to reinforce an integrated mind-set and the need to have all areas of the business contributing in tangible ways. Despite the significant changes that big data, social, and mobile have created within the business itself, this basic rule of business has not changed.

The following questions will help you adopt a proper perspective on how traditional financial analysis can be used to segment your digital community. Since these segments will rely upon profitability, and its revenue and expense components, as the basic rule to create them, it is important that they are compared to the traditional channels the organization uses to go to market. And, it is also important that they be compared equally—credited using the same rules to apply revenue and debited using the same expense categories and allocation methods.

- What is the cost to acquire new contacts? What percentage of new contacts are also prospects, and what is the difference in acquisition cost between a new contact and a new contact who is also a new prospect?
- What is the cost of each new consumer who self-identifies to the organization? Again, when are they and are they not prospects, and what are the acquisition costs associated with these two different groups?
- What is the cost to your organization when it must uniquely identify a consumer? What percentage of identified customers are actually prospects and what is the cost to identify each of them as opposed to consumers who are not valid prospects?
- What is the revenue per transaction for new customers? And the margin?
- What is the revenue associated with customers who are upsold or cross-sold and the margin?
- What is the revenue generated by customers during their relationship with the organization, and their customer lifetime value?
- What is the cost of contacting and identifying an influencer? How many consumers within this influencer's social community actually became prospects and customers, and what is the value of each of those customers (this provides a rough estimate of the financial worth of a one influencer versus another)?

When this analysis is performed for each channel it will quickly become obvious that motivating consumers to behave in ideal ways—self-identifying as opposed to the organization uniquely identifying them—is much cheaper and more efficient, and makes each customer more profitable. This financial analysis will reinforce the value of an integrated mindset, demonstrating how digital initiatives can impact every area of the business positively and tangibly.

Now let's look at an even more meaningful way that integrated enterprises use information to uncover profitable patterns and segments within their communities.

THE BASICS OF SOCIAL SEGMENTATION

Integrated enterprises think differently about how they analyze, understand, and use their social communities; they do not rely solely on traditional techniques exclusively. They adopt techniques that mirror how social consumers think and act.

Traditional analysis, which is heavily influenced by financial analysis, relies upon averages: average revenue per transaction, average cost to acquire new customers, or average customer lifetime value. When viewed across channels this tells leadership where they are getting the most bang for their buck, where they should place additional resources or seek to make improvements, and often shapes their strategic approach to the market. As a by-product of this approach the organization thinks in terms of averages, means, counts, and deviations to explain the performance of the group from which the average has been taken. Comparing one average, trend line or bell curve to another provides insight into which direction the organization should go.

This is a foundational approach to analytics—segment or sample a data set, calculate an average, compare it to other averages and decide on the next best step—and is therefore hard to change. It is also integral to statistical analysis—the foundation of modern analytical techniques—and therefore reflected in most analytics technology. It also supports a top-down mentality that managers are comfortable with: segment the business by channel and calculate averages to know which performs best, then segment that channel by product, brand, geography, sales person, or other important criteria and calculate averages to know which areas are best and worst; continue until the required insight is gained. This top-down analysis segments the organization's customer and consumer communities and allows them to make fact-based decisions.

It is at this point, the point of execution, where the logic of traditional analysis flies in the face of what makes Big Social Mobile enterprises more successful than their segregated counterparts. Integrated enterprises understand that profit is created by convincing one individual consumer after another that they will find value in the company's products and services. Therefore, analysis must start at the level of the individual consumer; it cannot be top-down (though companies obvious must be adept at both). A segregated approach follows one logic: What is my most profitable segment so that I can apply more of my resources to that segment? An integrated approach also uses a much different one: Who is my most profitable customer so that I can get more consumers exactly like that one; or, and how do I get everyone else behaving like my most profitable customer? Averages, while used, are less importent; and when they are, they are seamlessly attached to granular transactional information so that the root cause can be investigated; data sets are not sampled; summation remains connected to details. This type of analysis is hardly a mathematical exercise at all.

Remember, one of the major distinctions between a traditional and social consumer is that a social consumer expects to be treated as an individual during every interaction with organizations they choose to patronize. Whether it is a sales associate in the aisle of a retail store, a customer service agent on the phone or a consultant selling in a boardroom, the interaction that convinces a social consumer to buy will always be more successful when it is personalized. The individual customer focus that Big Social Mobile enterprises have keeps them more closely aligned with a social consumer's expectations, and allows them to adopt processes that rely upon personalized interaction to make them more effective. (It is important to note that while modern marketing techniques, such as predictive marketing, that rely on personalized messages to create this connection may seem the same, for Big Social Mobile personalized messages are only they beginning. Big Social Mobile enterprises are designing entire processes around the ability to interact with consumers in a personalized way across any channel.)

This is the mentality that forms the basics of social segmentation and analysis—what is sometimes called a "like-kind" or a "look alike" analysis. It takes one ideal customer, or more often a small group of customers for each channel, and seeks to find others who are the same, thereby facilitating (1) improved targeting, because the organization knows what appeals to them; (2) increased profitability, because they are converted more quickly and more often; and (3) increased effectiveness, because they are likely to be part of a social circle of other consumers much like them.

Recognize that you may encounter challenges with this alternative analytical approach. It can be difficult to identify enough consumers exactly like the perfect customer; the more specific your criteria the less similar target consumers are available. Be prepared to relax your definition of what a perfect customer is so that you can identify consumers that are nearly perfect. At the same time, be aware that these nearly perfect consumers must still behave in ideal ways because these behaviors led to superior financial performance—or rather, it is the task of your organization to get these nearly perfect consumers to behave in ideal ways. This will allow your organization, over time, to identify and appeal to increasingly profitable consumers within an increasingly profitable social community—again reinforcing that financial measures, while not providing equal insight as other forms of segmentation and analysis, are still the principal guiding factors for the organization, including the digital initiatives within it.

Integrated enterprises analyze their customer base in a variety of ways in order to find more consumers who are like their perfect customer—techniques that allow them to broaden their definition while still targeting consumers most likely to adopt ideal behaviors. The following sections describe these techniques. First, though, use the following questions to segment your community based upon this basic technique. This analysis might seem similar to the exercise used to segment your community under traditional financial analysis, but remember, social analysis relies upon finding the one perfect customer within a segment, not the average performance for each segment.

- For each channel, product line, or other key segment of your business, who is your most profitable and therefore most perfect customer?
- Who is your ideal customer based only upon the initial purchases, and then again based upon customers who were upsold or cross-sold additional products or services? Which customer is most profitable or ideal when viewed at each of the critical moments of segmentation versus total customer lifetime value?
- Given that the same customer will not be ideal at each critical moment of segmentation, who is the perfect customer overall? How does this fit with the organization's strategy—its short- or long-term approach to the market or average customer lifetime value versus the perfect customer's customer lifetime value?

BEHAVIORAL ANALYSIS

Your organization must become adept at analyzing the behavior of prospects, customers, and influencers to identify the interactions, or pattern of interactions, that led up to the preferred outcomes. This is called behavioral analysis, journey-mapping, or pathway mapping and analyzes the consumer's movement from one critical moment—the six key points of segmentation—to another. Once your organization understands the ideal pattern of interactions that connect each critical segmentation point, you can analyze other critical moments in this same way. For now, though, recognize that focusing on the critical moments helps you pay attention to behaviors that clearly add value.

Behavioral analysis covers a wide range of interactions. You may discover, for instance, that when prospects take a given action, it moves them closer to the point of conversion 75 percent of the time, or, when prospects take a different action, they will continue to investigate options but rarely buy. These actions show companies how to react and improve their processes. For example, it is now a common marketing practice to customize a series of emails, texts, messages, or advertisement placements for a customer based upon specific behaviors or interactions. This personalizes the interaction (beyond personalizing it with just an individual's name, title, or other explicit information) and reinforces the brand's presence, its products or services, in ways that are similar to the traditional push marketing techniques. While this approach is more effective than previous, impersonal contacts, it still reflects a segregated mind-set.

Integrated enterprises use behavioral analysis to be proactive. For example, much has been made of the social consumer's tendency to use mobile technology to view competitive pricing while in-store (often called "showrooming"). This behavior can cut both ways. The retailer with the consumer in their store can monitor the usage of a consumer's mobile device to understand what competitive mobile applications they most frequently use to perform this search and in some cases even monitor the search terms used and pages viewed. Over time, the retailer can provide their sales associates with this information, modify their pricing, or create signage and advertisements that counters this behavior. The retailer can now understand, more clearly than ever before, exactly who and what they are competing against. To combat this response, other retailers can "geofence" their competitor's stores—using technology to monitor when prospects enter and how long they remain there. This behavior can be combined with the information they are getting from the consumer's mobile device, competitive information available on the web, and feedback from their social community to craft messages, mobile offers, and discounts to win these consumers back.

The company that understands the consumer the best, and has done a good job of integrating all aspects of their organization to proactively modify consumer behavior, will be most effective in the market. [See Figure 8.2]

Behavioral analysis can also be used in a more complex way to understand intricate patterns that lead to ideal behaviors. In this application, organizations prompt consumers to learn one more small fact after another that cumulatively help the consumer reach the conclusion the company seeks, maximizing

Integrative Shopping Experience
(example)

Figure 8.2 The interactive shopping experience in action. How integrated enterprises cross the physical and digital landscape to understand consumer behavior, counter competitors and use information to maximize the chances that they will elicit profitable behaviors from consumers.

revenue or margin over the short or long-term. This more complex effort can include the following actions:

- Identifying how and when consumers interact with social communities and influencers, prompting the input of influencers at the right time.
- Setting mobile triggers that dynamically generate content based upon factors such as:
  - user behavior
  - sales people that contact the customer personally at exactly the right time
  - exposure to value-added content that beats the competition during the final stages of making a decision
  - customer service representatives who are tied into the sales process and know the right options to offer
  - operations personnel who perform their job in a way that best positions the customer to be upsold or cross-sold

This is behavioral analysis that will help you interact with consumers more effectively. It will use specific interactions and patterns of interactions, short-term situations where customer-facing employees can make decisions on-the-fly, and long-term scenarios where entire processes, applications, websites, and even product and services offers are redefined to solicit ideal behaviors.

All of this is made possible by the information contained in data—big data—combined with traditional information and put into the hands of the right employees throughout each function of the Big Social Mobile enterprise.

To begin using behavioral analysis to understand how consumer interactions are helping or hindering the achievement of ideal behaviors, use the following questions:

CUSTOMERS

- What journey—all of the individual interactions—did each ideal customer identified for each segment make as they transitioned through each critical point of segmentation? When viewed from a behavioral perspective—the prospect converted to a customer most quickly versus the customer with the highest initial purchase—which customers become the new ideal customer? Which customer is most closely aligned with the company's ideal behaviors short and long-term? What do the patterns of interaction look like for each of these different customers?

- Does the identity of the ideal customer change at each segmentation point? If so, what behaviors caused this change and is there another, different customer that becomes ideal when behavior is analyzed across multiple segmentation points?

- Which interactions most frequently achieve the desired outcome, and which most frequently prevent it? Which of them need to be more consistently utilized, changed, improved or removed to be more effective? Which interactions, when grouped at different levels, are most effective?

- What people or organizations had the most influence over customers during their journey, who did they trust most during the buying process and what interactions reinforced or detracted from this?

PROSPECTS

- How frequently are prospects conforming to the most effective patterns of previous customers?
- What sections of their journey most often delay prospects (from becoming customers) longer than the ideal customer? Are there interactions that are present or missing that trigger these delays?
- Where are the points at which prospects who never become customers most often depart from the typical path that customers take? What patterns most often became dead ends?
- What patterns of interactions most often and most quickly led consumers to self-identifying or to provide critical pieces of information, such as bridging data that allowed your company to uniquely identify them and therefore target them as prospects more effectively?

INFLUENCERS

- What interactions are influencers having with the organization and which ones solicit positive or negative responses?
- When are influencers engaging with the company in the physical world, and what interactions cause them to be willing to engage in deeper, more meaningful conversations? When these occur, how do influencers use these interactions within their community and what created a positive response?
- What content are influencers creating that has the greatest reach within their social community and which interactions, if any, assisted influencers in broadening their reach?

SOCIAL ANALYSIS

Like-kind analysis can also be used in another way that may be familiar to you; social and mobile practitioners rely on it because it is enabled by social media platforms themselves. All major social platforms now make available (often for a fee) information about each community member's demographics, their social connections, relationships, pages, posts and organizations they follow or comment on, those they most frequently engage in and other information about their preferences and personalities. All of this can be used to understand a consumer's social behavior. This information is so extensive that social platforms and other technology are able to categorize consumers not only based upon this information itself, but also based on what this information suggests about their personality types, their values, and their hierarchy of needs. This, combined with the geospatial information common to mobile data, is what actually makes big data so big.

In turn, integrated organizations combine this information with sentiment analysis—measuring a person's attitude, favorable or negative, toward a brand, product, or other topic. To determine sentiment, unstructured data—information contained in text fields, sentences or narrative form that does not have a clearly defined data model behind it—is analyzed to determine how likely a person is to respond favorably to an interaction. Organizations can conduct this analysis even if they are not actively participating in the interaction, such as when a person makes a comment on the quality of service they just received on their personal social feed.

You can use this analysis to find prospects that most closely match the social behavior or profile of your ideal customers. The better match someone is to the organization's ideal customer, the more likely they will respond in-kind to the same value proposition, branding, and interactions. This type of targeting is being used when companies apply different "hashtags"—a way of categorizing the topic based on its social message—to their social posts. Consumers will follow or monitor hashtags related to their interests, giving companies a way to interact with them even though they might never have made contact with them before. Like any other social information, an organization can learn what hashtags should be used or monitored by analyzing the behavior of their ideal customers, prospects and influencers—or competitors.

Integrated enterprises can also use social analysis to uncover new segments to which they can market based upon the social, political, cultural, or other affiliation or belief that the organization has. Companies align themselves with trends, such as homelessness, bullying, hunger, or pro-democracy demonstrations, using this analysis. If the organization is actively supporting a cause, they can post content about their participation to their social feeds, engaging consumers who are also interested in a given cause. This exposes a wider range of consumers to their brand and eventually their offerings.

While this is a valid and effective method of penetrating new markets, the organization must be committed to the cause and be well informed about it, since insincerity will alienate or damage the brand.

Use the following questions to help understand how your organization can use social analysis to improve the percentage of prospects, customers, and influencers behaving ideally:

- For customers, what are the interests, websites, organizations, social groups and other social behaviors that define your ideal customer in each segment? How narrowly defined is each type of behavior when compared to other customers from that same segment; which behaviors can be relaxed and by how much, to include more customers while still being narrow enough to be effective—what is this range?

- For customers, how does their social behavior change prior to and after each critical point of segmentation? How do these behavioral changes influence their value over time and at each point of segmentation?

- When subsegmenting customer groups based upon social behaviors, focus on the subsegments comprising consumers who became customers the quickest, who generated the most revenue or margin, and who took the least effort compared to the average and other groups. What do these subsegments look like?

- For prospects, how closely do their social behaviors match up against the behaviors of ideal customers? Is there a match between prospects who are more actively engaged with the brand and those who are more likely to buy? Are those prospects that have for all intents and purposes become inactive less like ideal customers?

- When reviewing prospects based upon the source from which they came, is one group more closely aligned with the social behaviors of your ideal customers than others? How can they be subsegmented so that they more closely align with ideal customers?

- What is the social behavior of social influencers? Does it vary for those who support your organization versus those who do not? Can influencers be subsegmented in a way that reveals social behaviors that make them more likely to behave in ideal ways?

GEOSPATIAL ANALYSIS

Traditional geospatial analysis relies upon plotting customer-related information, such as location, on a map so that the organization could decide how to best use its resources—locations for new facilities, best routing for vehicles, area grouping for sales territories, or where to hold meetings. This is common because many companies are predominantly concerned with efficiency; consumer behavior is often of little concern if it does not involve interaction with or use of a company asset.

Big Social Mobile enterprises use geospatial information for broader purposes. They believe that their organization must be able to track a consumer wherever they go, across both the physical and digital landscape—where they interact with your organization versus your competitors, where they go to understand the markets that you compete in, where they meet with those who influence them, or where they most often check-in. The area of concern could be as big as a sales territory or as small as the coffee kiosk in a convenience store, as public as a social platform or as private as a members-only group.

Therefore, they figure out how to reach consumers in any of these locations so that they are constantly reinforcing their same brand message across mediums—advertising both in the physical world (because social consumers check-in there and respond positively to cross-media marketing) and the digital world (because customers, prospects and influencers frequent certain digital locations in combination with physical locations). Geospatial analysis helps foster this integrated approach. When organizations can identify where consumers are both physically and digitally, they can tailor their interaction to include not only the right person interacting with the consumer at the right time, but also the right place.

This allows a brand to do many things: steal a customer before they enter a competitive location, or while in it; steal a dissatisfied customer when they leave the competitor's location (by stepping in when a consumer posts a negative review for example); associate their brand with a consumer's favorite locations by timely and coordinated delivery of messages; take advantage of consumers who are in locations where they typically have free time to view extended content, such as watching videos waiting for the train or sitting on a bus.

Use the questions below to see how geospatial, or location-based, analysis can help you understand how to get consumers behaving in ideal ways:

- Where are your ideal customers located across both the physical and digital landscape when they interact with your organization? Do they generally follow a sequential path through these locations or do they frequent these places throughout their decision-making process? What journey is actually ideal and leads to the most preferred behaviors? Do certain places have greater influence?
- In what locations visited by your customers does your organization maintain a presence? And how does your presence in these locations compare to your competitors and those who are influencers? Where you do have a presence, how extensive is it?
- How does the geospatial behavior of prospects compare to that of customers, especially when prospects are grouped based upon those who are still active and those that have gone stale? Are there places that speed up or slow down their decision-making process, or bring them to a dead-end entirely?
- In each of the locations that your prospects, customers and influencers frequent, how available is the *right* person from your organization? Will they be able to interact with the person most knowledgeable and able to maximize the interaction, those who can properly deliver the message that the organization wishes to deliver, and the one who can provide the most consistent, personalized experience possible?
- How aware are you of consumer behavior when they are in your competitor's locations—both physical and digital? Can you influence them when they are in these locations?

DEVICE ANALYSIS

Similar to geospatial analysis, most device-related analysis has to do with how effectively mobile technology is used to get consumers behaving in ideal ways. I'll discuss in greater detail how companies can use mobile technology to achieve integrated goals in the upcoming chapter specifically on mobile, but for now, let's look at a range of devices—smart phones, tablets, and laptops as well as wearable and smart devices (such as smart light bulbs)—that gather their own usage data.

All of these devices provide automatically generated data or information to those who want it (and in some cases are willing to pay for it). Because the data is automatically generated it offers advantages that traditional enterprise data (created by employee-influenced processes) and big data (some of which is automatically generated but all of which is consolidated, analyzed and distributed by employee-influenced processes) do not. It is typically consistent in structure and complete in scope. It tells those who use it everything about behavior relative to its usage. A smart light bulb will detail each on and off. A smart car will detail every mile it covers relative to every internal function that is monitored. A smart kiosk will detail every consumer interaction, sometimes including a photograph of the user and even—believe it or not—their fingerprint and biometric scan.

This device-related information helps companies understand the smaller details regarding many of the interactions they have with consumers. Not only can they make sure that the content they send each consumer electronically is properly formatted, they can infer personality traits, behaviors and beliefs, and derive moments of availability when that consumer is most likely to respond ideally.

Answer the following question to learn how analysis information from devices can help you get consumers behaving in ideal ways:

- Is all of the content sent to users properly formatted for the individual device of the user receiving it? Does your organization have a presence on every device being used by ideal customers that is specifically tailored to that device?

- What devices are being used by ideal customers? How wide is the variance on types of devices being used by ideal customers? Does the type of device have any impact on ideal customer behavior or is it only the information about usage patterns that holds value to your organization?

- What applications or platforms are being used to interact with your organization via mobile devices? What other, competitive or complimentary applications are also on those devices? What are the patterns of usage among your ideal customers, and how closely do your prospects match this behavior, especially when prospects are divided into active and inactive?

- What third-party devices would provide additional insight into the behavior of your targeted consumers?

THE ANALYSIS ADVANTAGE

Big Social Mobile enterprises are constantly searching for new segments and patterns that provide insight into how they can get consumers to behave in more ideal ways. But the expertise to identify and understand these ideal behaviors comes from many different employees in many different places throughout the enterprise. It is often not the social and mobile practitioners that create innovative tactics based on the patterns that are discovered but the Marketing, Sales, Operations, R&D, and other professionals who have the business knowledge necessary to capitalize on what the company has learned.

The key to taking advantage of the information contained in enterprise and big data is effective analysis—combining many different types to uncover profitable patterns and segments. The ones explained throughout this chapter are a result of new techniques and technologies, but they should be combined with traditional forms of analysis. Market-basket analysis, for example, shows which products and services most often sell together and can generate the highest revenue and margin. Cross-sales and upsell analysis reveal which products and services should be offered in combination and are most effective at generating more revenue from each customer. Customer churn and attrition analysis identifies which customers, moments, or factors contribute to the loss of customers. Next-best analysis (sometimes called "predictive marketing")—very similar to the behavioral techniques discussed here—uses predictive modeling to identify what actions are most likely to achieve the desired outcome.

Becoming proficient at all types of analysis is essential. It creates a competitive advantage for Big Social Mobile enterprises. They use the results of this analysis to gain insight into what is working to generate customers, increase profitability, and operate more effectively; to understand what causes influencers to be more favorably engaged with the brand, to glean product development suggestions from customers, to forge alliances with partner companies that operate as extensions of the enterprise.

For Big Social Mobile enterprises, this analysis forms the very foundation of both tactical and strategic execution, and is also used to set objectives and the strategic approach to the market. While segregated organizations might also use analysis to fashion tactics—they respond to posts, emails, or phone calls, they offer information and they change the types of posts they create—they do so only within siloed functions and do not use the information derived from their analysis for larger business defining decision-making. But Big Social Mobile ideal cannot be achieved, the results of all of this analysis cannot be put to use, if the organization itself—its people, processes, technology, and information—is not properly aligned to uncover these opportunities and take advantage of them. This is the focus of the next step in becoming Big Social Mobile.

Chapter 9

ALIGNING DIGITAL INITIATIVES WITH THE ENTERPRISE

AS IMPORTANT AS IT IS TO UNDERSTAND your community and your interactions with them, their ideal behaviors, and profitable patterns, your organization must be prepared to take advantage of these relationships and behaviors when they manifest, or better yet, force them to manifest, molding consumer behavior to these preferred patterns. This will not occur unless your digital initiatives are properly aligned with your organization.

In some cases this means sending the right message—either an automated or a manually generated message—to the right consumer, while in others it means ensuring that the right person within your organization connects personally with a consumer. In addition, these interactions must occur at the right moment—or more specifically, at the time when they are most likely to solicit the preferred response or ideal behaviour from the consumer. All three of the following criteria must be met for every interaction: the right person from your organization connecting to the right consumer, at the right time.

Proper alignment makes this possible and also ensures that all employees—knowledge workers, managers, and even executives—are working together to create a consistent consumer experience across channels, to deliver a consistent marketing and sales message, and to react consistently to changes in the market. This not only provides today's social consumer with a personal and consistent experience each time they interact with your organization, it also maximizes your chances of soliciting ideal behaviors.

In some cases, the action your organization will take is simple—it will send the most appropriate product advertisements when a consumer visits your website; a customer service agent will provide the information that best satisfies a customer during a phone call; the same customer service agent will proactively ask for additional information to better understand or identify the consumer; or the same agent will suggest exactly the right follow-on action that will move the consumer closer to the point of conversion. In other instances, you'll want your social media analyst to respond to an online comment that directs an influential consumer to the appropriate digital resource for insight into how the company's products or services are superior or perhaps you will direct your public relations manager to place a personal phone call when you first detect that a consumer is becoming influential, inviting them to an event and starting to build a valuable long-term relationship.

All of these interactions—and the myriad of others that Big Social Mobile enterprises engage in—require the integration of diverse data, diverse skills from different personnel, and diverse technology from different initiatives seamlessly woven into the enterprise. Information, derived from big data, must be woven into traditional enterprise data, delivered to employees who work in traditional departments, but who will often require the assistance of social, mobile, and big data practitioners to interpret and perhaps even respond through social and mobile channels. At the same time, these big data, social, and mobile practitioners require the insight, experience, and knowledge from traditional departments to interpret the information and behaviors they are seeing online. To make this possible, you must align digital initiatives with the traditional enterprise itself—not vice versa. Your organization must integrate them into your core processes, people, technology and information, in a way that facilitates and makes these Big Social Mobile behaviors possible.

This is the next, and final, step in becoming Big Social Mobile.

THE PROCESS OF MANAGEMENT

Information, when used properly, can create alignment. Without it, it is impossible to ensure that digital initiatives are helping the organization achieve its larger objectives. But to do so, the right information must flow between the right people, at the right time.

Integrated enterprises often use information to understand their relationships with different consumers, to see the gap between their behavior and the preferred ideal, and to help employees throughout the organization understand what they must do during each individual interaction. In this way, information aligns execution across the enterprise to keep a consumer's experience consistent.

But information also provides much larger insights—new market trends visible across social media can improve the effectiveness of sales and marketing processes, feedback from personnel in the field can improve the efficiencies enabled by mobile apps, and slight changes in online content can solicit consumer opinions that prompt new product and service offerings. It can provide tremendous insight into whether all of these things are occurring, are effective and efficient, and are generating the profit you are held accountable to create.

Used in this way, information makes possible what I call the *process of management*.

Enterprise data and social or mobile data—big data—are generated as a result of each interaction the organization has with a consumer. The digital fingerprints left behind by each of these interactions provide the foundation upon which all analysis occurs. Managers use the results to make decisions about how the organization should interact with each individual consumer. They see what is working and what isn't, and adjust accordingly; they attempt to make each interaction more effective. This is the process of tactical execution within an organization.

At the same time a much larger process is taking place (or should be)— something akin to strategic execution. Information also drives this process— information merged together to provide one seamless view across both the physical and digital landscape.

This process follows a set pattern: management asks a business question; employees design a process to answer this question; technology is employed to execute the process; and data is generated as a by-product, stored, combined with other data, and transformed into information that answers the original question. This process happens over and over, at different levels and points within every organization. In high-performing organizations management is fully conscious of this process and constantly seeking to ask better questions that drive their organization toward better answers that drive better bottom-line results, creating more effective and efficient processes and improving technology.

Managers use this process to understand how effective promotion campaigns are, to reiteratively improve them based upon the market response to offer the lowest discount and still capture the highest volume. They also use it to set pricing, stock the appropriate amount of inventory, offer additional incentives, and improve the content of social media posts, thereby increasing their reach, number of followers, sentiment, and engagement. They also use it to improve long-term processes, such as shifting their value proposition, their sales approach in different channels, and product portfolios and banner strategies. It is the process of continuously improving the organization.

To generate tangible and improved results over time, your organization should master this "process of management."

To accomplish this, information must be integrated *vertically* through the organization, from the lowest level, where individual subject-matter experts such as social media analysts, individual sales people, manufacturing floor supervisors, channels managers or customer services agents operate, to executives.

This is done by rolling information up: consolidating it from its smallest granule—an individual unique interaction between your organization and a consumer and the data that describes it—to the sum of all interactions that take place within each of the segments uncovered through the different types of analysis (financial, behavioral, social, geospatial, and device). This approach helps management make decisions from an integrated perspective, using all departments and levels of their organization (which includes information from their digital initiatives) to improve strategic execution, to keep management focused upon adapting and interacting more effectively with consumers, and to remain ahead of their competition.

However, when using information to align the organization vertically you will encounter two obstacles:

- Most managers solve problems from the top down. They break problems into generalized segments or key issues or major challenges and then pull each of those apart, seeking to understand the larger issue by understanding its individual components. They do this because the details are overwhelming and the solution must work to satisfy many different customers, products or channels. Unconsciously this approach causes them to find the best solution that will work the majority of times—the average likelihood of success highly influences their decision. This makes integrated information—the combination of traditional and big data—inherently difficult for some managers to include in their decision-making process. For example, the top-down thought processes will lead management to analyze which channel is most profitable and therefore where they should place the most resources to capture the most customers, revenue or profit. This will make it challenging for them to follow and accept the logic of identifying their one, perfect customer (often defined as their most profitable customer) and how redesigning an entire channel or process around that one customer can maximize revenue or profit. This will seem counterintuitive.

- The way information is reported in segregated organizations mirrors this top-down approach. Since digital initiatives are separated into their own silo from the very outset, it is difficult to see the impact they are having or might potentially have on traditional business performance— decision-makers rarely even consider factoring this information into their decision-making process, and standard reporting reinforces this segregated mind-set. This means, for example, that management often cannot understand the long-term financial impact of adapting processes around their most profitable consumer(s) because traditionally this information is commonly displayed in ways that do not even allow for the calculation of this approach—calculating the financial impact of changing processes to create more ideal customers is itself too challenging to allow management to analyze these changes using fact-based information and not conjecture.

To overcome these obstacles, your organization must make a commitment to gather and deliver information in a way that reflects the impact of digital initiatives on traditional business functions. Something as simple as showing the number of sales leads that come in via social or mobile channels on sales reports, or the number of customer queries that Customer Service handled as a result of social or mobile posts on operational reports is a good starting point.

With the basic information derived from this data, management can ask the next better question in a way that integrates these initiatives into the enterprise. Even if no new sales leads have come in via social media, seeing a zero in that newly added column of a standard report will force management to ask a logical, crucial next question: "You mean with over one million followers on social media we have not had one single new sales lead; why is that?" With this question, the process of management will have been started—as well as the movement toward becoming a Big Social Mobile enterprise.

Assess whether your organization is providing management with alignment-creating information by answering the following questions:

- Is information about the impact of digital initiatives (social and mobile) on traditional enterprise functions such as marketing, lead generation, sales, and operations included in information that is presented to process managers, heads of departments, and executives? Is information about the performance of digital initiatives from this perspective available throughout your organization?
- Is the performance of profitable segments identified through your social analysis reflected on management reports, side-by-side with the traditional structure of information used by your management team?
- Can information about the impact of digital initiatives on traditional functions be analyzed from summary level down to an individual transaction, customer, or interaction? Can this be done for traditional enterprise information or big data separately, and can it be done when this information is combined?

STRUCTURING DIGITAL INITIATIVES

Just as information must be integrated vertically to help you manage more effectively and guide the long-term direction of the organization, digital initiatives must also be integrated *horizontally* if the larger benefits that integrated enterprises seek are to be realized. Without horizontal integration, all interactions with social communities and individual social consumers are funneled through social and mobile experts; all big data is delivered back to these specialists and never dispersed throughout the enterprise to influence decision making.

While integrating information vertically puts information relative to your digital initiatives into the hands of executives for decision-making purposes, horizontal integration focuses on integrating digital initiatives themselves into the transactional processes of the organization. This allows the *right person* within your organization to take action and reveals how digital initiatives are aligned with the enterprise from a mechanical, process or tactical perspective.

The key to success is bringing resources from other areas of the organization—everyone from business leaders to a variety of functional experts—into the social and mobile conversation so that they can:

- Make sure that the right message is delivered. Working with social and mobile practitioners (be they internal employees or consultants), they can reinforce the core value propositions of your organization or its products and services and the differentiators that make you better than your competition. They can push conversations in a direction more closely aligned with ideal behaviors, preventing conversations from becoming unproductive. They can also shape consumer interactions to conform to profitable patterns and behaviors.
- Spot important trends that might have an impact on your organization's position in the industry, influence product or service offerings, expose weaknesses in key competitors, or identify opportunities to capitalize on events as they happen in real-time.
- Suggest creative solutions to consumer problems that haven't been previously thought of or internalize creative solutions within the organization when customers or consumers suggest them.
- Shape the thought process and discussions taking place within your company's social communities so that they are in your long-term best interests.

While these actions require treading on social and mobile practitioners' turf, those professionals lack the depth of experience that operations personnel, product developers, engineers, experienced sales people, and other experts have in these areas. At the same time, social media experts possess knowledge and skills that others in the company lack. Horizontal integration is about creating the right structure and processes that put the right person at the right place at the right time—to obtain the best outcome. When employees are held accountable to generate proper outcomes, they will overcome their initial reaction of sacrificing results to protect their own turf.

Organizations are often hesitant to open up their social and mobile processes to others in the organization. They've seen what can happen when Domino's employees post pictures of them defacing customer food; how Amy's Baking Company was exposed on social media by its owners Ray and Amy Bouzaglos, who, among other things, admitted to illegal behaviour; or the negative impact of an IRS employee tweeting that they were bad at math. While these types of disasters have occurred because non-social or non-mobile experts interacted with consumer groups via social media, as managers and functional experts have become social consumers themselves— and as organizations have given them training on how to engage in social media interactions—these disasters have largely become a thing of the past. When they do occur these days, they are the results of big data, social media, and mobile technology not being integrated into the very culture of the organization itself.

Horizontal integration is also important for another reason; it marks the moment in time when the organization truly commits to becoming a Big Social Mobile enterprise.

This commitment often does not change how these digital initiatives themselves are managed, but it will change how the big data, social, and mobile subject-matter experts interact with the rest of the organization. This interaction typically takes three forms, the last of which reflects the preferred integrated approach:

1. **Segregated**: No formal lines of reporting or processes connect digital initiatives to each other or to other processes, initiatives, or departments throughout the enterprise. Those responsible for digital initiatives interact with others to solve problems, gather content, or make decisions based upon the strength of their professional, and sometimes personal, relationships with employees throughout the organization. Therefore, the consumer experience will be inconsistent and disconnected from any larger business objectives.

2. **Centralized**: All functions related to digital initiatives are centralized into the digital initiative itself; multiple initiatives might be consolidated together but not into the organization at large. In some cases traditional

functions are duplicated within the initiatives, such as with the creation of "social customer service" but these functions are separate and segregated from their traditional counterpart and are not integrated into them. The consumer experience is consistent within one medium or channel, but will not be consistent across all mediums, channels, and both the physical and digital landscapes.

3. **Hub and Spoke**: All functions unique to the digital initiatives are retained within these initiatives and all traditional functions of the organization remain in their traditional location. Formal processes connect digital initiatives to each enterprise function into which they are then integrated. In the early stages, big data, social, and mobile experts act as conduits connecting these functions to social communities, but with time these conduits become unnecessary because employees and management within those functional areas develop Big Social Mobile skills. The consumer experience is consistent across all mediums as long as processes are adhered to.

To many organizations the centralized model may seem preferable since it allows the company the greatest control over its social messaging. However, it comes with significant additional costs (since traditional functions are being duplicated, adding additional people, processes, and technology to the organization) and it still does not provide the consistent experience that social consumers demand, nor does it create the integration that ensures the larger business messages are properly communicated. It could be considered a more sophisticated form of the segregated approach.

In contrast to this, the "hub-and-spoke" model seeks to keep the core functions of big data, social media, and mobile technology within the departments that manage them (typically IT, marketing and IT or Operations, respectively). This model disperses the information gleaned from big data in the same way that traditional enterprise information is distributed throughout management, integrates social media usage throughout a wider user base across the enterprise, and connects mobile processes to their traditional counterparts. This means that big data, social, and mobile subject-matter experts are still using and controlling technologies unique to their initiatives. Digital marketers, for instance, still manage social platforms and remain responsible for their subject-matter tasks (building social communities), but they are also responsible for supporting the usage or integration of their initiative within various traditional business functions.

Consider engagement. In a fully realized, Big Social Mobile enterprise, the organization can create significantly greater engagement when subject matter experts from throughout the business—the people who truly understand consumer needs and how the company meets them—engage directly with consumers. The current practice of having a social media expert responsible for engagement maximizes control, not engagement itself, and is less likely to get consumers and customers to behave in ideal ways and produce tangible results.

The hub-and-spoke model is sometimes compared to matrix management or a matrix organizational structure because the big data, social, and mobile specialists themselves are interacting with many people. As with matrix management, hub-and-spoke models of integration work best when enough individuals in influential positions have moved beyond the dotted-line debate of who reports to whom and strong executive direction creates a clear understanding of organizational (and therefore departmental) goals. When this type of culture exists, cooperation, teamwork, and communication result, allowing these specialists to help departmental leaders achieve their goals using the extra resources that big data, social media, and mobile technology bring to the table.

The hub-and-spoke approach also helps overcome the common belief held by many employees that those outside of digital subject-matter-experts cannot benefit from digital initiatives or use them to shape interactions with consumers in a way that yields tangible value. Big data, social media and mobile practitioners also fail to grasp these concepts. Installing the hub-and-spoke model, therefore, helps change employees' attitudes as well as their actions—it creates alignment both operationally as well as cognitively.

To gain an understanding of how well your organization is positioned to achieve the hub-and-spoke approach, answer the following questions:

- When a consumer (a potential prospect) first makes contact with your organization via social or mobile technology, what is your response and who in your organization responds?
- When a consumer is clearly a prospect (when they are showing obvious intent to purchase) who, if anyone, from your organization then takes

that lead and is responsible for closing the sale? Do employees responsible for social media or other digital initiatives usually interact with this prospect, or do you have processes in place designed to secure the involvement of someone from the sales department?

- When a customer shows additional interest in products or services via a social or mobile interaction, how is it handled?
- When customers state that they have a problem with a product or service via social or mobile, who responds? Does the customer problem go to Customer Service or Operations; does it stay within the social media initiative; or is there no response at all? Is the person who responds best able to solve their problem?
- Are there product improvement suggestions on any of your social or mobile feeds? If so, did this information make its way to someone who can use it? Was it used in any way to benefit the organization?
- When an influencer makes a statement relative to your brand, who responds from your organization? Are these responses helpful to the influencer and do they seek to build a longer-term relationship that will benefit both the influencer and your organization?
- When employees from your organization respond to opportunities or problems presented through social media, is your organization responding efficiently and effectively? How often are duplicative functions required? Are these handled via standard processes or informal relationships?

CONNECTING THE CUSTOMER JOURNEY TO THE ENTERPRISE

Creating alignment between digital consumers and the enterprise is complicated by the fact that consumers have minds of their own. They prefer to follow their own path, solicit advice from influencers with which the company has no relationship, and engage in behavior that delays their progress and carries them away from the ideal journey. And there's another complication: Moving consumers along on this ideal journey requires that you coordinate the efforts of many different employees in many different departments, making sure they work in concert to achieve this end.

To meet these challenges, your organization must have the ability to respond at critical moments—moments where your organization intervenes to send an individual consumer down the ideal—the most profitable—path. Without this capacity to respond at critical moments, your organization can observe and analyze but fail to take meaningful action.

PetCareRx, a leading online pet products retailer, was struggling to move its customers down the most profitable path. In just over 15 years they had become one of the most successful pet pharmacy and product suppliers by using standard techniques: a strong product portfolio, competitive pricing, and creative marketing combined with superior service, clear vision, and thorough understanding of their market and the passion of their consumers to care for the pets they loved. Fortunately, this understanding allowed PetCareRx to see the changes in behavior as their customers became social consumers. They quickly realized that if they did not respond they would begin losing existing customers and margins at an alarming rate.

Their solution was twofold: a change in methods supported by new technology. First, they adopted an integrated mind-set. This change relied, in large part, upon a redefinition of what "marketing" meant to the organization and an integration of marketing (the department in charge of many of their digital initiatives) into other organizational functions. Second, they changed their "one-size-fits-all" marketing and sales approach so that their interactions with individuals and groups of customers were aligned with the personalized approach social consumers were demanding, while at the same time helping solicit preferred behaviors: reduced attrition, improved revenue and margin, increased purchasing frequency, and greater loyalty. Achieving these outcomes would require information generated from both traditional data (where customer orders and products are detailed) and big data (where consumer behavior, preferences, and demographics are recorded). Once combined, this would provide the insight they needed to understand current behavior and how to influence it.

To accomplish this, they partnered with AgilOne, a predictive marketing platform that provides insight into customer behavior so that organizations can interact with individual consumers in a highly personalized manner. At first they focused on proactively reaching out to customers to influence prescription refill rates just before their pets' prescriptions expired. This soon evolved into customized offerings to specific customer segments, allowing them to do away with a uniform calendar of discounts and promotions for all customers. They then tested various offerings, incentives, and information combinations

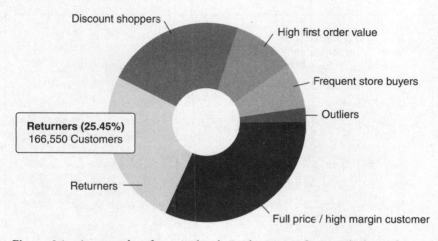

Figure 9.1   A screenshot from Agilone's Predictive Marketing Platform showing how consumers can be classified based upon their behavior.

on different behavioral segments to understand how various interactions and patterns of interactions impacted customer lifetime value, average order size, order statistics, campaign response rates, and other key metrics (see Figure 9.1). Eventually this allowed them to understand an individual consumer's propensity-to-buy, allowing them to offer only the minimum discount necessary to solicit the ideal response [see Figure 9.2].

The results were impressive: 38 percent year over year quarterly sales increase, 24 percent increase in net profit, 14 percent increase in quarterly retention, more than double the expected value for ROI and campaign response rates, and a zero percent increase in spending for promotions, discounts, or overall marketing budget. PetCareRx had figured out how to use their digital initiatives to not only improve the effectiveness of their customer-facing processes, but also to achieve a competitive advantage.[1]

"Marketing is becoming more customer-focused because companies are realizing the value of their company is the sum of its customers," says Omer Artun, CEO of AgilOne. "Marketing has been the first function to focus on who customers truly are—comprehending their behavior, what motivates them and identifying and acting on root causes to improve customer metrics. This approach and strategy will eventually permeate to other departments, such as finance, operations, merchandising, and customer support in a similar step-wise approach. It all starts with metrics that serve this purpose, understanding

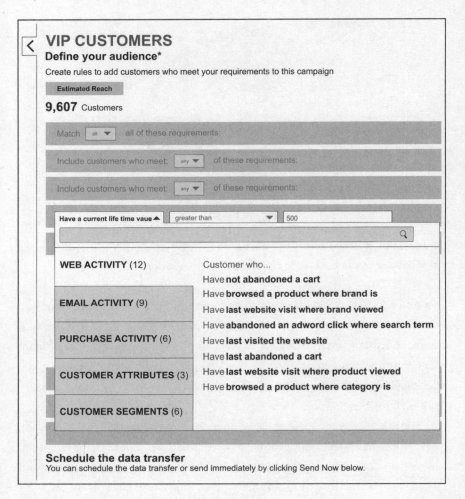

Figure 9.2 A screenshot from Agilone's Predictive Marketing Platform showing how consumers can be specifically targeted based upon their behaviors.

levers that improve these metrics and focusing on exceptions to solve issues and double down on successes."

Social consumers want their journey to be aligned with the enterprise. As consumers become more engaged with your company, they believe that your social and mobile presence should be more than just a corporate marketing tool or even a way to converse; they believe that it should be a portal giving them access into all aspects of your organization and meeting their needs. But this creates challenges for organizations because social and mobile platforms are not designed to connect directly to an organization's native platforms or technology. That gap must be closed by an integrated process, combined with technology and employee interventions.

Consider how customers think when they have a problem. Typically, they seek help by returning to the employee with whom they had their original interaction—the retail salesperson, the account representative, or customer service agent, in person or via phone, email, or web. These employees are often not responsible, qualified, or empowered to solve the customer's problem, and yet in high-performing organizations, when this unhappy customer is referred to a different employee or department, they feel understood and cared for; they don't feel like they are dealing with separate departments, that one hand doesn't know what the other is doing.

Analytical technology facilitate processes that allow different employees throughout the organization to have a consistent view of consumers, helping them understand the consumer's situation when they come into contact so that consumers believe that employees have talked to each other, even though one is a sales associate standing in a retail store, one is an overseas customer service agent, and one is a social media expert. These technologies achieve this goal by allowing different people within the organization to understand where the consumer is on their journey through the organization—from the moment of first contact until they eventually leave the organization behind.

To understand whether your organization is guiding consumers properly, answer the following questions:

- Is your organization able to respond with a unique message to each individual prospect that you come into contact with based upon an analysis of his or her social, geospatial, device, or other behaviors and their demographics? How quickly can these responses be sent and how personalized can they be?
- How effective are your organization's personalized messages at changing prospects' behaviors to more closely match your ideal patterns or behaviors?
- When during the prospects' decision-making process can your organization intervene to change the course of their actions and how effective are these interventions? What effect do these have on increasing the number or speed of prospects that are converted to customers? Does this have any effect upon the value of their initial purchase, their likelihood of being upsold or cross-sold and their lifetime customer value?

- How successful is your organization at intervening in the decision-making process of a buyer when they have selected to purchase from a competitor? Are you able to intervene digitally or at their physical locations?

- When consumers contact your organization, is each employee in each department that interacts with them able to see important information about these consumers, the value they represent, and their prior interactions? Can each of your employees clearly understand what next consumer behavior they should be seeking to elicit and how to do so?

- Is your organization able to interact with consumers in a way that improves the softer aspects of relationships with customers: improved satisfaction and loyalty, more frequent mentions or recommendation via social media, increased engagement that leads to product improvement suggestions or market intelligence?

- Do your consumer interactions steer them toward processes that are naturally more effective and efficient for your organization? For example, when and how do you direct consumers toward your mobile applications and digital resources?

SENTIMENT, ENGAGEMENT, AND MANAGING RISK

There is a whole world of consumers out there beyond just those that have identified themselves or that your organization has uniquely identified—the prospects, customers, influencers, partners, and potentially even competitors that your organization is interacting with. Rather than dismiss these unidentified consumers as segregated organizations do, integrated enterprises can create alignment even with these unknown groups. By discerning who among these groups are important to their organizations and inserting themselves into conversations between these consumers, they can uncover new prospects, influences, partners or competitors, shaping their behavior and market opinion.

To capitalize on this unknown but valuable group of consumers, you must understand how important your brand is to consumers within broad social communities (sometimes reflected in "engagement" metrics) and what their feelings are about it (called "sentiment"). This has long been a focus of social practitioners, used as a means to gauge the effectiveness of their efforts to build and engage communities. Big Social Mobile enterprises do this as well, using engagement and sentiment to understand these same things. However, they also use them to align their digital initiatives with their enterprise, making sure the right person within their organization is aware of what is happening in the market, allowing them to intervene at critical moments.

More specifically, integrated enterprises create alignment by taking the following actions:

- Connect an engaged consumer to the right person within their own organization who has the proper knowledge to influence the consumer's sentiment (typically a prospect or an influencer) or lead them toward more profitable behaviors.
- Identify those consumers (most often prospects or influencers) who are not engaged with the brand, but should be, and then connecting them to the right person within their own organization. This is often based upon the consumer's interests, social circle, or demographics.
- Identify consumers with poor sentiment so that the right person from within their organization can reach out directly to these consumers to address their concerns and hopefully improve their sentiment.
- Identify groups of consumers who have needs or share interests relative to the brand so that they can be converted to prospects or influencers but also so that these groups will multiply the organization's reach and influence.
- Identify new influencers as they begin to gain influence (often by tracking their Klout score) so that the organization can shape their opinion and behavior; or find consumers with a positive sentiment (toward the organization) to steer them toward the preferred behaviors of influencers.
- Uncover new topics (often through the use of tags or hashtags) that could be relevant to the brand and could be used to extend the brand's reach or influence.
- Intervene at the right time, either to manage risk by spotting potential problems while they can still be contained or opportunities that can be exploited (which might include exposing a competitor's problems).

All of these actions revolve around the ability to identify and influence a consumer's engagement and sentiment, either for an individual consumer or the market in general, and to intervene at the right time. Technology can help organizations accomplish these tasks. The story of how this technology evolved illustrates why it has become so crucial to create proper alignment between consumers and organizations.

For over half a century, PRNewswire has been connecting organizations to the media via press releases and formal announcements. But in 2009 they saw the market shifting. Informal information being exchanged via social media was gaining influence over brand opinion; formal quarterly financial statements were no longer influencing consumer opinion as strongly; and brands could no longer understand, let alone control, market opinion based solely upon corporate-media relations. In response, PRNewswire introduced technology that eventually became its current Agility platform.

Agility allows organizations to monitor conversations across all mediums— across traditional media such as newspapers, magazines, television and radio, and also across new media such as websites, blogs, e-zines, and social media platforms—dispersing formal press releases across both the physical and digital landscape so that an organization's message is consistent. It also integrates this formal, often highly crafted messaging into the less formal communications occurring via social platforms, blogs, and other online media outlets. This allows the organization to mass distribute information (the original purpose of press releases) and then understand the market response. They can then refine their content and approach to solicit the response they desire, at both a broad level, and within specific demographic segments. This creates a feedback mechanism for how they position themselves in the market.

But this isn't enough for integrated enterprises. Agility also allows organizations to drill down into sentiment and engagement—all the way down to individual consumers and individual comments or posts on any public social media platform or community area. This means that an organization can now fully integrate their marketing into Sales, Operations, R&D, and any other departmental functions. Organizations can literally connect any employee directly to any consumer on any platform and deliver a one-on-one or group message about any topic. In integrated organizations, these communications are personal, personalized, and value-based because the employee interacting with consumers is the one who can best influence their engagement and sentiment, and can best steer them towards profitable behaviors. Sometimes this will be the social media expert, but often it will not.

Organizations also have the ability to target any topic they choose. While it is common to monitor one's own brand and product names, it is also common practice to monitor competitors, notable influencers, partner organizations, or topics that represent a threat or an opportunity. And this monitoring can be routed to various functions and levels throughout the organization, putting information and the ability to act in the hands of a diverse group of employees in key business functions. Just as companies can use geofencing to influence consumer behavior and opinion within a competitor's physical locations, this technology allows them to utilize a similar approach based upon combinations of tags, keywords, topics, companies and specific usernames.

As I've noted, some worry about allowing a disparate group of employees or managers to interact with digital consumers, fearing they'll say or do the wrong thing. Using this type of monitoring technology, however, reduces this risk, providing internal control over social conversations.

To assess whether your organization is properly positioned to monitor sentiment, engagement, and risk, answer the following questions:

- How many employees, either knowledge workers or management, are able to interact directly with consumers of any type through social or mobile platforms? What departments or functions are they from within your organization?
- Have you set up a process where big data, social, and mobile practitioners can call upon other resources/functions within the organizations when they need them?
- Do employees from different departments and functions have the ability to monitor interactions occurring through digital mediums so that they can intervene when necessary?
- How have consumers behaved when interacting with people from different departments or functions? When do these interactions lead to preferred or ideal behaviors, what new responses do they elicit from consumers, and when are they most and least effective?
- Is there a feedback mechanism in place so that your organization understands the market response to formal communications delivered to traditional and digital media? Is this feedback distributed to management

and influencing future go-to-market strategy? Does this feedback mechanism also provide insight into informal responses to your organization's content? Does this feedback influence go-to-market strategy?

- Does your organization have the ability to intervene during consumer conversations with both individual consumers and groups of consumers? On what platforms? On what platforms is this intervention most effective?
- Does your organization monitor consumer sentiment across the market as a means to manage risk and spot opportunities? How effectively have you mitigated risk and seized opportunities when identifying them?

*   *   *

The real power of properly aligning digital initiatives is to dynamically multiple the reach and influence of your organization to an increasingly broader audience and opening up new market segments that could not be otherwise reached. This allows the proper person to craft the right message, sometimes delivered personally and sometimes by technology, to the right consumer or groups of consumers at the right time. And yet, all pieces of the organization are working in concert to deliver a consistent experience for the consumer and a consistent message into the market.

Proper alignment also allows the organization to respond more proactively. When big data reveals startling trends about how consumers are responding to an organization's content or interactions, Sales, Marketing, or Operations can change the message or approach; when sentiment and engagement reveal a sudden opportunity to enter a new segment or capitalize on a competitor's weakness, senior management is able to quickly take action; when specific consumers have complaints, suggestions, or insights, a social media specialist can immediately engage in the conversation. Proper alignment enables the integrated enterprise to take action—to solicit ideal behaviors, to solve problems, and to implement a process of constant improvement grounded in factual information. At its core, the multiplicative effect of an integrated approach allows organizations to get results for the money they are already spending—bringing these new tools and techniques to bear where those who are most responsible for the performance of the organization can use them to create tangible business value.

Part III

CAPITALIZING ON THE CONNECTION

IT IS ONLY A MATTER OF TIME before every television pays closer attention to the people it is watching than those who are watching it—not just their viewing preferences, but also their responses, facial expressions, behaviors, clothing—even their biometrics.

Chapter 10

CAPITALIZING ON THE MOBILE MOVEMENT

AS YOU READ ABOUT THE PROCESS to become a Big Social Mobile enterprise, you probably noticed that more space was devoted to social media and big data than to mobile technology. Though "mobile" is also the third word in this book's title, neither its placement nor the space allotted to the subject should be taken as suggesting that it is of tertiary importance. Rather, it's a result of a lack of the current business sophistication when utilizing mobile technology. While organizations have become more astute about the business advantages of big data analytics and social media strategies, they are still in the early stages of understanding how to fully leverage the power of mobile technology. As a result, relatively few good examples of an integrated approach to mobile technology exist. While organizations may spend a lot of money developing a technologically sophisticated mobile application, this expensive app is often pedestrian from a business standpoint.

Organizations need to integrate mobile technology into their core business process and strategies, and into their big data and social media initiatives. I've referenced how companies such as Starbucks have done so successfully, but we're just starting to see organizations wake up to the huge business potential of mobile technology, and it's time that more business leaders capitalized on this potential.

MOBILE HELPS FIGHT CAVITIES

Once every six months I get a text from my dentist telling me that I'm due for a check-up. The office phone number is hyperlinked at the end of the text. When the text comes in, I always click the link calling their office attendant and schedule an appointment. According to my dentist, over 70 percent of her clients do the same exact thing every time they get that same auto-generated text message.

This simple application of mobile technology is significantly more effective than many of the thousands of expensive mobile applications developed by companies and corporations each year. My dentist's use of mobile helps her overcome two of the standard business problems in the dental care industry: providing a repurchase reminder without regular patient contact, and overcoming buying inertia because no obvious need to repurchase exists at that moment. When dentists fail to solve these problems, customers often do not get both of the cleanings typically authorized by insurance companies each year. My dentist estimates that over 30 percent of her patients fall into this group. Her usage of mobile has nearly cut this in half. If her dental group has 1,000 patients who fall into this category, she is able to recover $85 per visit over $85,000 per year—plus the revenue from other products and services that customers could be sold during the extra visit.[1]

Now consider the significantly larger revenue loss for a major corporation that fails to capitalize on mobile technology. Companies suffer tangible losses when they fail to get customers to behave in ideal ways using mobile—both the obvious cost of developing unprofitable mobile applications and the opportunity costs that occur when customers are doing other things with their time and money.

These costs are not obvious to most companies because mobile technology emerged from simple cell phones and was therefore designed from the perspective of a personal user. First impressions last, and people perceived smart phones as personal technology that should make their lives easier, simpler, more efficient, and more fun. As a result, companies developed applications largely focused on personal entertainment and personal convenience. By the time businesses got around to adopting it as a business platform, mobile had become synonymous with personal usage, and this influenced how companies developed their mobile applications. Most companies followed one of three paths:

- Develop the simplest application possible, making only limited customer interactions available to minimize development costs.
- Create as extensive an application as possible, allowing consumers access to product catalogs, customer service, purchase, and payment features and as many other parts of the business as possible.
- Create an application that has little to do with the mainstream business, but is entertaining, thereby building brand goodwill.

Each of these three approaches lacks an integrated mind-set. Rather than craft a mobile strategy based on core business objectives, these approaches segregate mobile from the business. Each fails to use mobile to conduct business in a more meaningful and profitable manner. Instead, mobile should be viewed as another channel through which companies can interact with consumers and do the things businesses have always done—marketing, selling, servicing, and supporting them. As you will see, because of mobile's power, integrating it into the business should be the mantra of every organization.

THE MOBILE CHALLENGE

While consumers may not realize the extent to which their mobile devices provide organizations with insights into their personal lives, organizations too often possess little understanding of what they can learn and how to use this knowledge. Mobile devices deliver deeper insight into a single user's behavior, decision-making process, and personality than any other technology available.

Most organizations are aware of the basics—if a consumer downloads a company's mobile application, the company will know who they are based upon their login information. If the application's login is a social login, the company will also get all information that the consumer authorizes this application to receive, which may include personal details as well as their social network and often their behavioral information. However, organizations are often denied a great deal of information about consumers because social platforms can either fail to capture all the information that companies might want or might choose to not make all of this information available.

As a result, integrated enterprises build data collection functionality into their own mobile applications, just as they build appealing interactivity. This interactivity, or functionality, sets the foundation for what data will be made available to the organization. At the very least, to facilitate proper data collection the mobile application should do the following:

- Allow the consumer to interact with the company through chat, email, and/or phone
- Implement automated processes that allow orders to be placed, status to be tracked, or help tickets to be submitted
- Establish ecommerce or other payment methods
- Give consumers the ability to submit information to an organization in various ways, including, for example, using a camera to automate check deposits, or to gather information that they need, such as using a camera to collect data or plot their location on a map
- Offer a means to respond to surveys or provide additional information to a company that the company needs
- Launch loyalty programs, advertisements, discounts, or other incentives that appeal to consumers but are actually provided as a means to get the consumer to behave in specific ways.

This functionality will be combined with a social login, so that the organization has access to social and behavioral information, as well as the standard information relative to the device itself and the relevant geospatial information. Integrated enterprises design this functionality to not only facilitate interactions between consumers and their organization, but also to collect the information necessary to define the relationship between the consumer and the organization properly, to understand each interaction between them in granular detail, and to match them up against their perfect customer and preferred behaviors.

Integrated enterprises then use this information in an unexpected way. While their application appears to operate passively in the background, it is actually managing the process which determines how the company will interact with the consumer. Their applications collect data, analyze it to determine where the application's user stands relative to the organization's ideal behaviors, profitable patterns and the profile of their perfect consumer, and then creates an automated response (or prompt a manual one) that determines when and what type of information will be returned back to the consumer via any medium. The user's response to this information then starts the process over again with the goal of moving them ever closer to an ideal outcome. This is a repeated, iterative process facilitated by the mobile application itself (sometimes while interacting with other back-end technologies).

Big Social Mobile enterprises, however, can be even more aggressive and innovative in how they incorporate mobile devices into their business strategy.

Personagraph, a mobile platform provider and developer, provides mobile applications and application add-ons that help its clients collect information about consumers via mobile devices and customize the user experience; their technology utilizes data drawn from the device to match the user against a company's perfect customer profile (a "like kind" analysis). They are then able to personalize and deliver advertisements and mobile content and even change the look and feel of the application itself to fit that particular user's interests and demographics. This helps companies gain a more intimate understanding of their consumers and modify the application in real time to solicit more profitable behaviors.

The benefits of this highly integrated approach include:

- Engaging the consumer more effectively using highly targeted notifications
- Timing notifications to appear at specific places the consumer is visiting across both the physical and digital landscape—their home, gym, retail stores, or retail websites
- Timing notifications to appear when the consumer takes certain actions, such as opening specific applications or remaining idle for certain periods of time
- Launching cross-media notifications that can tie mobile content to emails, web browser advertisements, digital product placement, or other digital devices
- Determining how demographic and social interests influence usage and how these can be leveraged to monetize behavior
- Linking personal interests to the content the consumer receives so that content delivered is tailored to appeal to that specific consumer—i.e., if a person likes the outdoors or a certain animal, the background of an application can adjust to feature these items

SAMPLE INTERESTS*

- Action Games
- Adventure Games
- Antiques & Collectibles
- Arcade Games
- Automotive
- Beauty
- Board Games
- Business/Finance
- Camera/Photo
- Card Games
- Casino Games
- Computer Games
- Consumer Electronics
- Cooking
- Deals
- Dice Games
- Education
- Fashion
- Fitness
- Food / Grocery
- Games & Toys
- Gardening
- Health
- Health/Medical/Pharmacy
- Magazines

- Movies
- Music
- News
- Outdoor Activities
- Parenting
- Pets
- Politics
- Pregnancy
- Puzzle Games
- Reading
- Real Estate
- Religion
- Restaurants/Cafes
- Role-Playing Games
- Self Help
- Shopping & Retail
- Simulation Games
- Social Networking
- Software
- Sports
- Sports Games
- Tours & Sightseeing
- Travel
- Travel/Leisure
- Trivia/Games

*Not comprehensive. Actual Personagraph taxonomy contains over 500 interests.

Figure 10.1 A sample listing of the over 500 interests that Personagraph can track based upon social information.

This type of integrated approach allows organizations that use technology, such as Personagraph, to understand their application's position and usage on a consumer's mobile device relative to everything else the consumer does on that same device. This means that they can tell if their application sits on the highly valued "front screen" of a mobile device, or if the user has buried it in a folder on the last screen they have to scroll, signifying that the application is not an integral part of the consumer's life, has little mindshare, and is likely to be deleted. They can uncover patterns of device usage, digital behaviors, and physical activities that trigger certain positive or negative outcomes for the company. They can also identify a consumer's preference relative to over 500 different interests, shaping content, products and service in ways that once seemed unimaginable. [See figure 10.1]

With this functionality, integrated enterprises can compete for social consumers even while they are standing in a competitor's store, prevent showrooming in their own, or pull them from a competitor's website. It becomes one more way—an important way—that they solicit ideal behaviors. This approach also provides much of the data—the big data—that integrated enterprises need to categorize their digital relationships, understand interactions, profile their most valuable customers, and match consumers against them. In the end, mobile applications provide much of the information that allows companies to understand the value of a consumer who is using their mobile application to connect to their enterprise.

MOBILE EMPOWERS EVOLUTION

Thinking about mobile integrated into the business has another advantage: It helps overcome some of the problems that digital initiatives first created for companies. The Internet, and then social media, removed many consumers from the physical world where companies could see and touch them. It gave consumers anonymity and private communication channels that helped them seize power in the corporate-consumer relationship. Mobile, if approached correctly, can shift the balance in a more equitable direction.

Although mobile phones are digital devices connecting the consumer to the world around them using a digital tether, the smart phone itself exists in the physical world. Consumers realize this when they lose it. They can log onto a website or call their service provider and find out exactly where their device is located. For social consumers, times when their device is lost are the only times their device is not physically with them. This tracking mechanism, though, is always on, regardless of whether the phone has gone missing. Therefore, for the first time, companies always know exactly where consumers are nearly every time they are interacting with them.

Mobile devices, through a social login or a login connected to the company's infrastructure, also reveal the consumer's entire social network (typically by sharing the consumer's contact list or address book). Since most people travel in social circles with people who are relatively similar, companies can uncover numerous new prospects by mining information contained in their perfect customer's big data. The company can then quickly establish a relationship with any of these prospects that it has not already interacted with—without the original customer knowing. Companies that have integrated this information with their enterprise data, and have included geospatial data, will also know, with relative accuracy, the location of the consumer's entire social community, and the location of any customers and prospects that exist within it. The company can now see and understand the behavior across both the physical and digital landscape (and multiple spheres within the digital landscape) and need only modify their internal processes to provide the seamless experience social consumers expect.

Creating a consistent experience is also made easier because mobile devices are easily connected to the enterprise. They commonly collect bridging data that is well structured and unlikely to change, directly connecting them to the company's data store that contains prospect and customer information. This allows a company to see and understand how consumer behavior is changing over time—not just their actions, but also their attitudes and opinions. Consumers often change, for example, their feelings based upon the economic outlook, which influences their propensity to buy, just as they change their stance on national or global issues, such as the need for organization to become environment friendly. Integrated enterprises use this to understand how brand positioning, product and service development, and marketing and sales techniques need to be adapted to remain effective.

Organizations certainly understand the value of mobile, but all too often they dilute that value by launching mobile applications that have little to do with their core business. Consumers will not spend their valuable and limited amount of time on an application that does not somehow provide them with information, knowledge, and even skills that they could not get anywhere else. Therefore, organizations should review their interactions with consumers to determine how a mobile application can make it easier, more effective, and efficient for consumers to interact with them. Individual interactions, or groups of interactions, can often be streamlined within a mobile application and allow the organization to collect data as a by-product. Social consumers, who understand that companies use applications to collect data, will not be offended if they believe they are trading their personal data for useful functionality.

As critical as mobile is to the success of integrated organizations, leaders need to guard against being swept up in the mania of reinvention. Though I've stated this warning before, I reiterate it here because I've just detailed the amazing knowledge that can be gleaned from a sophisticated business approach to mobile technology. A CEO may read it and think, "This is revolutionary! I need to change our business." It's easy to think this way, especially because at first glance many highly mobile companies seem as if they have revolutionized business itself. Looking below the surface, though, shows how they simply seized an opportunity to improve what already existed:

- Whatsapp didn't invent messaging, texting, emailing, or any other form of digital communication, but they did exploit a gap in the market that allowed people to message each other, even from overseas, using a Wi-Fi connection that allowed them to avoid texting or SMS fees.
- Hotel.com didn't reinvent how to sell hotel rooms; they saw an opportunity to sell rooms in underbooked hotels to travelers on-the-go—something that could only be effectively done using mobile technology.
- Rovio, the company that created Angry Birds, didn't reinvent their mobile game or their organization once they saturated their core market; they identified and penetrated new market segments by partnering with brands, such as Star Wars, that exposed them to secondary markets they could not have entered otherwise.

* * *

This approach—using mobile along with social media and big data to help an organization evolve to its next better form—relies upon a firm understanding of the organization's value proposition and an understanding of what the consumer would find most valuable (most easily done when an organization is consumer-centric). This must be combined with how an organization interacts with consumers and their ideal behaviors so that an optimal solution and usage of mobile can be achieved. Multiple people throughout the organization must grasp these issues so they can interact effectively with the mobile development team. In this way, their combined efforts can help create functionality that will appeal to the consumer and maximize mobile's value as a data collection device.

Chapter 11

DEMYSTIFYING BIG DATA

PERHAPS THE MOST COMMON MISUNDERSTANDING THAT segregated organizations have involves big data. Organizations routinely separate big data from enterprise information—they collect, store, and analyze big data in one place, enterprise information in another. And often, little coordination between data collection and information creation exists, either upfront in the design of the information/data management programs or afterwards in the analysis of what is received. Without this coordination, an integrative approach is impossible.

Just as a purely technological approach to mobile can become an obstacle to the integrated ideal, so too can this myopic view of information and data. Removing this counterproductive approach and demystifying the label that has caused such confusion and segregation can be done by adopting a different perspective—starting with the problem of the name itself.

AN UNFORTUNATE MISNOMER

Any other label besides big data would have been better: social and mobile data, consumer data, behavioral data, or even digital data. The right label (or a better label) would have given leaders an understanding of what purpose this data served and placed it in the proper context for them. Although other issues besides its misleading name exist, the "big data" label has created expectations about how the information within it should be handled, utilized, and thought about.

"Data" is the wrong word in and of itself, regardless of its size. Information is a more appropriate choice: social information, mobile information, consumer information, behavioral information, or even digital information. The use of the "I" word would allow organizations to compare apples with apples; it would encourage them to relate digital information to enterprise information, management information, or executive information. Information, unlike data, provides direct access to how consumers—social and otherwise—interact with organizations and the larger world.

This isn't just semantics. When organizations see digital and traditional information as part of the same family, they are able to more easily see the logic of merging the two into one information store that becomes a vital strategic asset reflecting organizational performance and consumer behavior across both the physical and digital landscape.

While we're stuck with big data as a term, we don't have to be stuck with the perspective it has imposed. To escape this mind-set, it's useful to look at how organizations launched big data initiatives—as segregated efforts focused on gathering, storing, and managing big data as an IT project.

DATA WAS ALWAYS BIG

Organizations often perceive big data to be separate from traditional enterprise data because it seems so large that the average organization cannot manage it and therefore cannot put it to proper use. Organizational leaders, under the influence of media hype and, sometimes, the influence of their internal IT specialists, expend time and resources debating how to manage it—as if managing data sets that are increasingly large is something new.

Yahoo!'s quick rise to Internet dominance was driven by this same need to manage overwhelming amounts of information. As the Internet expanded, Yahoo! created a new type of portal and search engine to solve this problem. But we can go back much earlier to see that this isn't a modern problem—technologists have endeavored for centuries to manage large amounts of information effectively.

When the First Congress of the newly formed United States set about to apportion the members of Congress relative to the population of each state, they had to figure out how to do something that was for them totally new. They needed a method to collect and analyze a large amount of data (the first US Census), a data set that turned out to be 3,929,326 people big—the largest number ever counted in the new world. This was clearly big data for 1790.[1] This was a sizable goal for a country that had just settled the revolutionary war, and had no idea how many citizens actually resided within it. Congress didn't debate their ability to perform a census count to the point that it derailed their efforts. Instead, they focused on the need to conduct it, the cost relative to its value, and the purpose the resulting information would be used for—all relevant business questions.

Eighteenth-century technologists later created technology to meet these business needs. Herman Hollerith, early technologist, created the electric punch card computer, the first ancestor of all computers.[2] Today's descendants of that first computer using new techniques to generating answers (relational queries, On-line Analytical Processing [OLAP], and in-memory computing) are all designed around the same approach: storing individual data points for use within larger, more complex calculations.

Even before there were actual numbers, data existed that was too big to be easily analyzed: *Big Data*. And technology quickly rose to meet the need. Business leaders today should take a lesson from our founding fathers: focus on the business issues that information can be used to address—focus upon the needs and allow the specialists to ensure that those needs can be met.

Just as the first computer was invented to meet the requirements of its time, today's technology and methods have evolved to meet organizational requirements generated by big data, and at relatively reasonable costs (costs that are rapidly declining with each new technology entering the market). Therefore, the discussion of size relative to big data is a distraction, sidetracking organizational with technology requirements rather than enabling discussion on what big data is necessary to meet management's needs, how it is best handled, and what is the most cost-effective approach. In fact, management and technologists should be having an entirely different discussion.

ENTERPRISE DATA VERSUS BIG DATA

Part of the reason that today's leaders often focus on the size of big data is because they do not clearly understand what information it contains. They understand traditional organizational data, knowing that at its core, traditional enterprise data is made up of information that relates customers to products—what customers ordered what products, what products the company should maintain and from which vendors, what was charged for each product ordered by each customer, and so forth. Many additional pieces of information are then bolted on to these interactions between products and customers as a business environment becomes more complex: what assets are used to move products to customers and at what cost, how many times sales people called or contacted a customer before they made a purchase, or how many people does the organization need to hire, train, evaluate and develop to be effective. Additional data then springs up around each of these new, more detailed needs (asset management, customer relationship management and human resources respectively) and is combined with the customer and product information contained in route accounting systems and enterprise resource planning applications.

For management, the connection between these business elements is clear. They know that if they want to understand the total cost to meet a customer's needs, they need to combine the cost of goods with direct costs and then allocate overhead. They can answer this important business question using simple facts and math.

But if you ask management how to calculate the value of one specific digital influencer with which the company maintains a relationship, they will have a significantly more difficult time—because the answer requires the use of big data combined with traditional data.

To understand how to answer this more complicated question, you must first understand how big data is structured and how it is fundamentally different from—but complementary to—traditional enterprise data. Recognize that the question of an individual social influencer's worth has two components: social and traditional. The social component consists of the new customers this influencer is connected to and how this influencer has influenced their behavior or decision-making process. The traditional component involves the monetary value of their contribution.

An integrated enterprise is able to determine the value of an individual influencer by analyzing the social community of the influencer and identifying the current customers who were once prospects within it. It can then determine the date at which these customers were converted from prospects and how this coincides with the point in time when the influencer began asserting their influence on the company's behalf. The current value of the purchases of these customers (or in some cases the average customer lifetime value of similarly profiled customers) determines the worth of the influencer. An integrated enterprise is able to refine this calculation even further, factoring in the influencer's sentiment and engagement to understand more precisely how much they were likely to have influenced these consumers leading up to their conversion.

In truth, the conversion of all of these consumers to customers probably cannot be attributed to this influencer—some of them would have become customers anyway. But the answer to the question of influencer's value does not need to be absolute. It can be relative, showing the value of one influencer relative to another, giving management the insight they need to make an informed decision about the value digital initiatives are adding to their organization—relative to the other ways that they could be using the organization's resources. Once management understands how to answer this type of question, they are much better able to integrate information contained in big data into their decision making process.

When companies integrate big data (to address the social component) and traditional data (to address the value component), they increase their ability to create information that will help them achieve business objectives. Segregated organizations often rely on big data to answer questions such as how many followers do they have, what are their common behaviors, or what triggers a positive response from them. But what management truly desires are answers to broader questions that end with a positive or negative impact upon traditional business measures. This can only be accomplished when the information in big data is taken a step further and tied back to (typically through the use of bridging data) the revenue and cost components contained within the enterprise itself. This integration creates a view of performance that more accurately reflects an organization's interactions with today's social consumers.

THE STRUCTURE OF BIG DATA

To identify the real value of an influencer (or similar complex questions), the entire organization must understand what data they can retrieve from social and mobile platforms, and what can be derived from big data. They must understand the structure of big data itself.

Social platforms make a significant amount of data available to organizations (some free and some paid for). This is the data used in the different types of analysis that Big Social Mobile enterprises perform to better understand and build closer relationships with their consumers. When data from these platforms are joined together (either in a company-managed data store or through third-party social login technology), each new consumer action creates a more complete picture of who that consumer is, the make-up of their social circles, their interests, their behavioral patterns and trends, and even their psychographic information. Organizations can achieve a more granular, detailed understanding of their perfect customers, creating a linkage between consumer attributes and how they are likely to behave—whether they are prone to ideal behaviors and how they react to each company interaction, pertinent news stories, advertisements, and other brand-relevant topics.

This distinction between what is relevant to the brand and what is not prevents organizations from becoming lost in the size of big data. Too often, big data practitioners collect all data possible, resulting in a quagmire of facts and figures. Overwhelmed, some companies respond by focusing on a narrow swatch of information; or they concentrate on the most accessible or easiest-to-understand data (i.e., number of followers). This, however, contributes to a segregated mind-set—little attempt is made to analyze this data with larger business objectives in mind. Management fails to ask important questions using this data—how are our social media efforts increasing customer value—and instead settles on using just a small part of big data.

Integrated enterprises, on the other hand, analyze the data from their social platforms in ways that combine sophistication with granular detail. Janrain, a company that uses social logins to provide its clients with a deeper understanding of their social consumers, can, for example, pull a significant amount of data from social platforms, making it and the analysis of it available to their clients. For example they can currently collect information relative to four major groupings, eight major sub-groupings, and over 35 individual data elements, plus core profile information, from Facebook. [See Figure 11.1] Twitter, on the other hand, only allows them to share relatively little information, only one major grouping, two sub-groupings, and five individual data elements. [See Figure 11.2] And they can do this for over 30 platforms, with new platforms integrated as they become more popular.

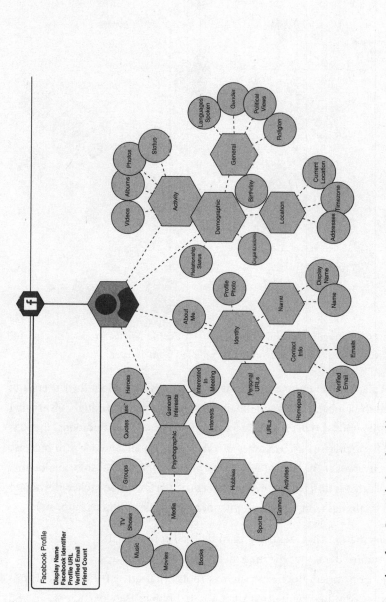

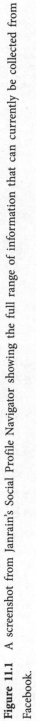

Figure 11.1 A screenshot from Janrain's Social Profile Navigator showing the full range of information that can currently be collected from Facebook.

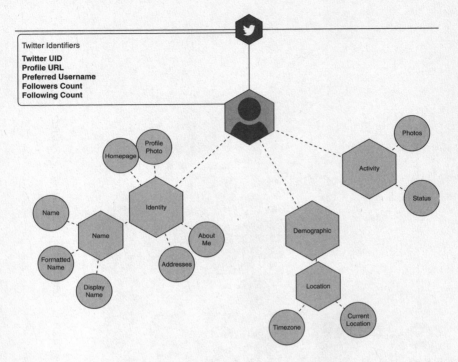

Figure 11.2 A screenshot from Janrain's Social Profile Navigator showing the full range of information that can currently be collected from Twitter.

Social platforms are prone to sharing more information about their users, not less, since these platforms predominantly generate revenue through advertising (which relies upon this data for its increased effectiveness over traditional marketing) and partnering with companies that need this actual data itself (to increase their effectiveness as Big Social Mobile enterprises do). While the information that can be collected is different for every platform, it can always be broken down into standard groupings (some of which will not be available on some platforms):

- Information that identifies an individual consumer
- Standard demographic information about the consumer
- The consumers' interests, such as topics that attract them, televisions shows or other media that they watch, hobbies they participate in and career paths they've followed
- Consumer activities relative to a specific platform (such as sharing of professional articles or sharing of personal photographs)
- The size of the consumer's social network on the platform

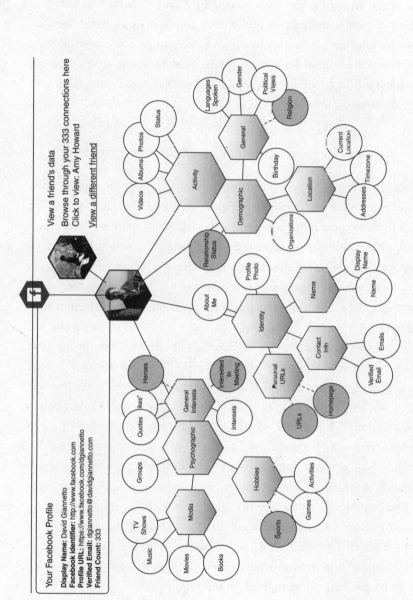

Your Facebook Profile

Display Name: David Giannetto
Facebook identifier: http://www.facebook.com
Profile URL: https://www.facebook.com/dgiannetto
Verified Email: dgiannetto@davidgiannetto.com
Friend Count: 333

View a friend's data

Browse through your 333 connections here
Click to view: Amy Howard

View a different friend

Figure 11.3 My profile as displayed though Janrain's Social Profile Navigator, showing what information is available based upon my Facebook activities (facebook/davidfgiannetto). Gray objects, where no connection exists to the parent object, reflect data that is not available based upon my profile and social behaviors.

When thought of in these more clearly defined terms, organizations can see big data as something that provides more insight into consumers as individuals, groups of similar individuals, and market segments as a whole. They can then analyze information in ways that have a direct impact on major business issues, answering traditional questions about consumers—such as the value of an individual influencer. But this is only possible if big data is integrated with traditional enterprise data.

INFORMATION, NOT DATA, GENERATES BIGGER CONTENT

Integrated enterprises value information over data. They determine what information is crucial to their business objectives, and then they pursue the data that fits into these objectives and yields viable information. Three questions will help you assess whether you are putting information before data: First, upon what platforms should you seek to build a presence? Although you may have a quick response from a data perspective, your answer could be misleading because social and mobile platforms are consumer-controlled technologies.

It is important to remember that consumers decide what role in their life Instagram will fill versus the photo-sharing capabilities of Facebook, or Twitter, or any number of new platforms that might arrive in the future. While it would be easy to say that Facebook is preferred (Facebook shares over 35 data points versus Instagrams' 7), it would actually be much easier to get consumers to share photographs of your products "in action" over Instagram because this more naturally aligns with how consumers have decided to use the Instagram platform. While organizations can gather more big data using Facebook, they would likely see more value using Instagram because they would be getting better, and more usable, responses (consumer engagement with this program would be higher). Understanding what information you are seeking, along with the business objectives, provides the proper direction for subject-matter experts who may then step in to focus on the data.

Second, how will you know that the information you receive from these platforms will be useful? Organizations actually don't know if the information they get will be useful—only what data points they will be allowed to gather. To some extent this is because organizations often forget that interactions via social media should be conversations. Sometimes you simply need to ask consumers for the information you need. By asking (for example, asking for photos of your product being used in creative ways), you get answers that are useful and insightful—often providing insight into questions that you would never have thought to ask.

Therefore organizations must focus upon using content (in the form of posts, questions, surveys, etc.) that will trigger responses that provide insight or even epiphanies. Used this way, content can fill in information gaps that the organization has, and help them understand how they can motivate consumers to adopt profitable behaviors. Focusing on the right content will be challenging for organizations following a segregated approach because social practitioners don't know what information different areas of the business need or will find useful and therefore do not know how to use content to solicit meaningful answers.

Third, if content is used to solicit information and is conversational by nature, how will you use this information since much of it will be delivered in unstructured formats? Organizations using a segregated approach won't be able to use a significant percentage of the information contained in the unstructured comments, posts, and pictures. While some technology can filter through this information to determine a generalized response from consumers (as is done to calculate sentiment), much of this information is too generalized to be used for any more detailed purposes.

Integrated enterprises use a simpler method. Since integrated enterprises disperse the usage of social and mobile information through a hub-and-spoke model, they are putting the ability to solicit these responses into the hands of the employees best able to analyze the resulting unstructured data—the response from consumers to the content posted. Consider something as simple as a product manager posting content that solicits consumer feedback on potential new features. Even by just skimming consumer response, the product manager will quickly gain more insight into consumer opinion than would be possible through even the most complicated, time-consuming survey. This can then be combined with the quantifiable data, such as consumer demographics and behaviors, to better understand what suggested new product features would appeal to the largest or most profitable or most influential group of consumers.

The answers to these three important questions all involve big data. But, little of the narrative comprising the answers to these questions has to do with data itself. This reflects the mind-set of Big Social Mobile enterprises. Information comes before data so that the minimum effort is expended capturing the minimum amount of data necessary—generating the maximum return.

Ultimately, information-savvy organizations will join the push to move ownership of these types of technology initiatives into the hands of business users (as opposed to its traditional ownership by IT professionals) and even to view the entire IT department as a service itself, billing out the cost of the department to users on an hourly basis. Business leaders are starting to take to heart the philosophy of information before data. While technologists may be loath to look at the relationship between technology investment and profit in such clear-cut terms, the leaders of business do not have this same luxury.

But one thing is certain. Data will continue to grow. What is big today will be even bigger tomorrow. Devices have become smarter and will be smarter in the future, and social and mobile platforms are collecting and sharing more and more data each day. Further discussion among today's leaders about how this bigger data will be handled will only serve as a convenient distraction from the more important questions I've posed here about how this information should be merged with traditional enterprise information to paint a clearer and more holistic picture of consumer behavior and business performance.

Big data alone cannot provide valid answers to the questions leaders are asking because it cannot show the impact of this behavior upon the profit equation. It is the difference between understanding the "cost per click" of a Facebook campaign and the cost to create a new customer via a social media channel. The first is anecdotal; the second represents tangible value.

Chapter 12

TECHNOLOGY TRENDS, BUSINESS IMPLICATIONS

THE PACE, DEPTH, AND BREADTH OF ENTERPRISE integration are only going to increase in the coming years. Organizations will find themselves spending more of their time and resources trying to connect the disparate dots between big data, social media, and mobile technology, between various functions and these three initiatives, between information and data, and between business goals and digital activities.

Increasingly, organizations will realize that making these connections is the key to success. They will come to see that being the first to market with a product or service, creating a splash with an expensive marketing campaign, or coming up with innovative methods, processes, and products are all secondary to an integrated approach. As important as all these tasks will continue to be, changes taking place in how business is conducted will make forging seamless links between disparate business tactics and strategies the number one priority for all organizations.

Technology is driving this trend. Consider how it's doing so.

BRIDGING THE PHYSICAL AND DIGITAL

Organizations are concerned that the power of online brands such as Amazon will make the in-store retail shopping experience obsolete for nearly anything that isn't perishable, highly influenced by impulse, or required on demand. They worry, too, that advancements in same-day delivery techniques may even cause consumers to buy impulse items online. Much of this concern, however, is fueled by the media hype that comes when Amazon introduces the idea of same-day delivery via helicopter, but it does make executives question whether they should attempt to reinvent themselves.

Online retailers do have some advantages: consumers can be more easily manipulated during the online shopping experience, data collection is significantly better, advertisement placements and personalization are more easily targeted, and the cost of modifying consumer behavior is cheaper. But no matter how good the "recommended for you" algorithms of an Internet retailer is, they will always lack a core value proposition that brick-and-mortar retailers retain: the feel of a pair of jeans when you try them on, the weight of a hammer when you hold it in your hand, the perfect shade of material that you can only know when you see it.

Online retailers also provide convenience, price advantages, consumer review information available at the click of a button, pictures and videos of the product in use, and other advantages. At the same time, some of these advantages are offset by the limitations of the online medium—it isn't convenient when something has to be returned because consumers couldn't hold it in their hands and try it out before they take it home. Online retailers also don't necessarily have a price advantage—physical retailers price-match all the time, just as they install video screens to show products in action and offer up consumer reviews. Physical retailers also are able to place a video screen in the hands of a knowledgeable sales person who can use it to provide shoppers with a more satisfying interaction than anything they could get by searching the Internet for answers to their concerns.

What companies with segregated mentalities forget is that despite the technology and the digital initiatives, the basic value of business really hasn't changed. According to a Motorola Solutions survey, 75 percent of US retailers believe that developing a more engaging in-store experience will be critical to their business in the next five years.[1] Brick-and-mortar businesses need to adopt the behaviors of their more consumer-savvy online counterparts. And when they do—which they will do because only the strong, only the integrated, will survive—they will find that the rules of competition really haven't changed: consumers, social or otherwise, determine value; those who provide the most value thrive.

In the future, all organizations will find themselves in a perpetual arms race to understand and meet consumer needs more efficiently and design processes that more effectively shape consumer behavior. Their ability to achieve this goal will center upon one thing: breaking down the barrier between the physical and the digital world.

TECHNOLOGY BREAKS THE PHYSCIAL BARRIER

In the not-too-distant future, your organization will possess astonishing capacities for learning about and interacting with consumers. Imagine every piece of glass that consumers looked at or through was looking right back at them. Your organization is able to "follow" consumers via computer screens, televisions, mirrors, car windshields, storefront windows and in-store displays, and eyeglasses. In the future, this glass will facilitate the organizational need to break down the barrier between the physical and digital.

Envision being able to send a text message or an advertisement via these communication surfaces that steers consumers to a nearby kiosk for additional discounts, directions, or information. The kiosk has already downloaded information about the consumers' mobile devices and matched this information to their digital profiles. The kiosk's content, the color schemes, and the items featured will all be automatically tailored to each specific consumer's preferences. Facial recognition programs will identify the consumer and scanners will identify their clothing, eyewear, and jewelry, instantly profiling the consumer. When consumers touch their screens to make a selection, it will read their biometrics and record these fingerprints and the unique arrangement of sweat glands on their fingertips, giving you the knowledge you need to solicit preferred behaviors from them.

Glass is becoming smart.

In fact, organizations should expect mobile device glass to become even smarter than it already is—smart enough to sense consumers' moods, mental states, how long their attention span is likely to last at any given moment, and even potential health problems. This information may seem relevant primarily to device manufacturers, advertisers, pharmaceutical, or healthcare companies—only those that can directly generate revenue from this interaction. But the impact will be significant for all organizations.

We are emotional creatures. We take actions and make decisions–love brands or hate them, purchase what sometimes doesn't make sense while we delay purchasing what we need—based upon these emotions. At very specific moments, our mental state combines with our physical state to make us vulnerable to messages that would otherwise not trigger an emotional response—just as we cry at the end of a movie on one day but remain unmoved on another.

Once devices have the ability to sense these moments of vulnerability companies will no longer interact with consumers based on geospatial, behavioral, or social analysis. They will target consumers based upon an *emotional* analysis.

Companies will compete for (and compete to generate) those small moments where they could bring the right person from their organization in contact with the right consumer, at the right moment with exactly the right message to connect *emotionally,* in order to get them to behave in ideal ways. This could be used overtly to detect when the propensity to buy is highest or more insidiously to reinforce or increase a consumers' emotional connection to a brand through subconscious responses. Biometric feedback, combined with behavioral, social, and personality analysis, will open an entirely new approach to selling: *psycho-sales.*

Organizations don't have to wait decades before capitalizing on some of these techniques.. This approach to understanding and using people's emotional and physical states, combined with an understanding of their behavioral patterns, historical reactions, and personality, is already possible. It is used in very specific cases to analyze and modify the reactions of athletes, astronauts and soldiers. Using it to influence the average consumer requires only the installation of relatively inexpensive technology. The first step of this installation has already been accomplished, in the form of the mobile device.

Once the second step takes place—embedding more psycho-emotionally sensitive technology into these devices on a widespread basis—companies will have taken back power in the corporate-consumer relationship and once again hold sway over widespread consumer opinion. Only this time it will not be based upon the influence of mass marketing, it will be based upon the power of micro-marketing—and the power of companies to integrate this information back into their enterprise.

ALL BRANDS WILL BE LIFESTYLE BRANDS

As important as this cutting-edge technology will be, integration in the future will require a broader organizational view, one that includes not only traditional aspects, but also includes less tangible considerations, such as elevating consumer sentiment to stategic importance.

Those things that social consumers have the deepest emotional connection with (measured as "sentiment" in the social sphere) influence all aspects of their lives: the brand of clothes they wear, the coffee shop they frequent, the luxury car they drive, the brand of golf clubs they swing, the makeup they wear, and the television shows they watch. These are also the brands they spend the most time searching for and researching online, the ones they follow on social media, and the apps they download to their mobile devices. Lifestyle brands have found a way to get consumers to follow them across the digital divide because they display an attitude or represent values or a passion that consumers identify with as part of their own personalities. This type of *sentimental* connection to the brand goes beyond simply intriguing consumers, entertaining them, or educating them.

In the future, all brands, even those that are thought of as mundane, will need to think and operate as lifestyle brands if they want to become market leaders. Some brands will attempt to do this using the current segregated approach that relies upon marketing campaigns to draw consumers in; others will do this by building hype around the new products and services they launch. But these approaches will see little long-term traction, and although they might increase sales, they will not create the deep emotional connection necessary to embed the brand into the rhythm of the consumer's natural daily life.

It may be difficult to conceive of a company that makes paper towels becoming a lifestyle brand, but if you had asked business leaders 10 years ago if a coffee company could become a lifestyle brand, most would have said no. Given the approach Starbucks took, with its highly stylized and personalized branding, it is easy to see how it happened. But consider that it also happened for Dunkin' Donuts, a company that was struggling to build a strong brand image until it used social media to clearly define itself and create a personal emotional connection to consumers.

Some companies create an emotional, lifestyle-like connection with consumers by associating its brand with causes that resonate more deeply than their products, just as Proctor & Gamble did by aligning their Secret deodorant brand with an anti-bullying campaign. Other organizations use the services of companies such as PRNewswire, aligning clients to major events such as the NCAA basketball tournament.

Whatever the tactic chosen, organizations will take communicating their business mission, values, and purpose more seriously in the future. They will integrate their core business proposition into not only their social and mobile content but also into every aspect of their business, every go-to-market strategy, and every employee's behavior.

Their corporate personality will then become what connects consumers to the brand, exceeding just the draw of its products or services. It will impact the way leaders think about the business. Executives in large companies are used to relying upon the power of their organization, its economies of scale, to dominate the market. They can operate over a larger area, reach more consumers and create greater influence among them, make up for inefficiencies with extra expenditure, and if all else fails, beat smaller competitors on price. All of these things are true—but they will not sway passionate social consumers.

Social consumers will go to extremes to search out companies that are most closely aligned with their own interests, beliefs, and values, and the Internet, combined with social media, has made them easier to find. This diminishes the competitive advantage that big brands and highly scaled operations have over smaller companies because smaller companies often possess a more personalized message that consumers can connect with. These smaller companies, too, are more willing than larger organizations to communicate their corporate philosophy and provide a more consumer-centric experience.

Certainly, large organizations will maintain a competitive advantage in the future, but they will need to use this advantage to:

- Create an understanding of their unique company culture among many more consumers than their smaller competitors reach
- Generate larger communities by creating deeper content that reflects their commitment to their brand image

- Use their resources to understand consumers be:ter
- Refine their messaging to be more on-point

By taking actions that integrate the company's vision with consumer perceptions, they are in a much better position to create more effective social initiatives and mobile apps, glean additional insight from big data, implement more effective internal processes, and execute creative, inventive strategies.

EMBRACING THE FUTURE

Advances in technology and methodology highlight how important an integrated approach will be to the success of companies in the future. Now is the time for organizations to embrace these changes with the same fervor that social consumers have embraced them—with the same fervor that so many of your employees have embraced them in their own personal lives.

You might look across your industry and see that these changes are not yet taking hold; you might not be inclined toward early adoption; or you might be an early adopter only in words and not in deeds. You also might believe that your current level of success is good enough or that you still have time, or even that the future I've presented throughout this book will never arrive. There are many ways to justify waiting.

But with your greater awareness of what is going on around you that this book has revealed, you should recognize that waiting or continuing with a segregated approach imperils your organization; that savvy companies are taking actions to integrate their initiatives today. At the very least, I trust that what you've learned has shifted your perspective, that you are now able to spot processes that remain segregated in only a physical or digital portion of the landscape and see technology that fails to unite them; that you look at reports and notice the gaps in performance and demand more insight, better information, and new data. With this fresh perspective, delaying will begin to seem difficult and dangerous. You cannot afford to wait until your industry adopts new Big Social Mobile behaviors; it takes only one integration-minded competitor to put you at a distinct disadvantage with social consumers.

Now is the time to take action to put your organization on the path to becoming Big Social Mobile. Here are some actions that every organization can take right now to capitalize on the technological and other changes that will affect them in the rapidly approaching future:

- Conduct an immediate assessment of whether big, social, and mobile initiatives are operating in relative isolation or whether they might already be showing signs of integration.
- Define what current resources you have to work with: people with digital skills that can assist in integrating digital initiatives into the business, processes that can bring together the physical and the digital, technology that will assist in these efforts, information that can unify performance and measurement across both the physical and digital landscapes.
- Survey the information you are getting from big data and determine its connection to enterprise information and business performance, viewing its connective nature from a top-line revenue and bottom-line profit perspective, from the market's perspective, and from the perspective of an individual consumer's view of your organization.
- Set traditional goals for your digital initiatives; give managers of traditional departments and functions goals and objectives that are more commonly found within digital initiatives, such as increasing engagement, identifying new prospects or influencers, or increasing the number of (positive) interactions with potential customers.
- Redefine how your digital initiatives can be measured in concrete business terms that reflect their ability to contribute tangible benefits to your organization.
- Foster a new cultural mind-set by creating integrated teams to reexamine segregated initiatives and provide cross-training so that traditional business functions and digital initiatives are working in concert to achieve the Big Social Mobile ideal.
- Bring senior management together to discuss your corporate identity, your beliefs, and defining principles, and how they can be more clearly communicated through social and mobile channels.
- Examine whether the company's larger social purpose is being conveyed through its social and mobile initiatives.
- Review the big data available to your organization and select only one or two specific points at which the integration of it into enterprise information and specific processes could create real value.

*   *   *

With these actions in mind, consider how they will position your company to take advantage of technological advances that are much closer than you might think. Consider the possibility that you can point a "smarter" phone at a broken appliance and it immediately tells you the part you need to fix it and gives you instructions for doing it yourself, and delivers the part to your residence within the hour. Imagine being able to summon a Customer Service Agent via a mobile application when you're having a problem, or better yet, how an insightful company might know to send customer service assistance (via any medium) before you even realize it's necessary. Sophisticated applications of technology designed to create an emotional connection between a brand and a consumer are powerful. These are the things we think of when we contemplate the power of new technology to change our lives.

But these outcomes don't just happen. They require an organizational commitment to integrating digital initiatives into the corporate fabric. It's not the initiative itself or the accompanying state-of-the-art technology that makes these visions a reality. It's the commitment to and the execution of an integrated approach. Organizations often launch digital initiatives that fragment their efforts and segment their enterprise. Those leaders who do a better job of integrating digital initiatives into their enterprise—their people, process, technology and information, their products and services—are seeing their organization rise to market dominance.

Big data, social media, and mobile technology will not be the last digital initiatives that require executives to rethink how their organization operates, the place it holds in the market and how it will deliver value. As I've suggested, the technology already exists that can turn every glass surface into an interactive provider of critical information and a brilliant communication tool—new initiatives will flow from this technology and others as it is developed and adopted by a growing number of organizations. Whatever the initiative, however, companies should remember that the measures of business success do not change, but how the game is played does. Integrating each new initiative into your organization can allow it to remain competitive, supporting and enhancing the value proposition that consumers have already come to respect—perhaps even helping it evolve to its next more powerful form.

Consumers have changed to become social consumers. Our economy has changed to become a new social economy. Organizations must change as well. They must become Big Social Mobile.

NOTES

1 THE INTEGRATED ENTERPRISE

1. http://www.berginsight.com/News.aspx?m_m=5.
2. http://www.mobileworldlive.com/over-7m-users-for-starbucks-payment-app.
3. http://www.ask.com/question/how-many-cups-of-coffee-does-starbucks-sell-a -day.
4. http://www.starbucks.com.
5. http://articles.chicagotribune.com/2005-04-13/news/0504130351_1_chain-of -coffee-shops-starbucks-blended.
6. http://www.mobileworldlive.com/over-7m-users-for-starbucks-payment-app.

2 BOTTOM LINE, MISSION-CRITICAL BENEFITS

1. http://socialtimes.com/how-dunkin-donuts-uses-social-media_b100752.
2. http://www.fool.com/investing/general/2014/01/13/dunkin-brands-increases -customer-engagement-via-so.aspx
3. http://www.dailyfinance.com/2014/01/13/dunkin-brands-increases-customer -engagement-via-so/.
4. http://www.marketwatch.com/story/dunkin-donuts-new-mydunkin-advertising -campaign-puts-real-fans-social-media-content-in-the-spotlight-2013-10-08.

3 OBSTACLES TO INTEGRATION

1. http://www.internetworldstats.com/emarketing.htm.
2. http://www.pcworld.com/article/155743/oldest_domains.html.
3. http://techcrunch.com/2009/08/27/25-years-later-first-registered-domain-name -changes-hands/.
4. http://www.verisigninc.com/en_US/why-verisign/education-resources/domain -name-industry-brief/index.xhtml?loc=en_US.
5. http://www.verisigninc.com/en_US/why-verisign/education-resources/domain -name-industry-brief/index.xhtml?loc=en_US.
6. http://smallbiztrends.com/2012/09/failure-rates-by-sector-the-real-numbers .html.

7. http://searchenginewatch.com/article/2299176/Why-Users-Delete-Your-Mobile
    -App.
8. http://www.google.com/googlefriends/alert2_2000.html.
9. http://www.wired.com/wired/archive/7.03/bezos_pr.html.

4   UNDERSTANDING THE NEW SOCIAL CONSUMER

1. http://www.cisco.com/c/en/us/solutions/enterprise/connected-world-technology
    -report/index.html; and http://www.prdaily.com/Main/Articles/90_percent_of
    _young_people_wake_up_with_their_smar_13466.aspx#.
2. http://pt.nielsen.com/documents/tr_200811_CSR_Fairtrade_global_report
    October08.pdf.
3. Jon Picoult, Watermark Consulting, "The Watermark Consulting 2013 Customer
    Experience ROI Study," April 2, 2013, accessed February 18, 2014.
4. Harald Weinreich, Hartmut Obendorf, Eelco Herder, and Matthias Mayer, "Not
    Quite the Average: An Empirical Study of Web Use," in the ACM Transactions on
    the Web, vol. 2, no. 1 (February 2008), article #5.
5. http://www.invodo.com/resources/statistics/.
6. Harald Weinreich, Hartmut Obendorf, Eelco Herder, and Matthias Mayer, "Not
    Quite the Average: An Empirical Study of Web Use," in the ACM Transactions on
    the Web, vol. 2, no. 1 (February 2008), article #5.
7. http://www.huffingtonpost.com/2011/06/29/myspace-history-timeline_n
    _887059.html#s299852&title=June_2011_Impending.
8. Kleiner Perkins Caufield & Byers's annual Internet Trends report.

5   UNDERSTANDING DIGITAL RELATIONSHIPS

1. Chuck Martin, *Mobile Influence*. Newyork, NY: Palgrave Macmillan, 2013, page 223.

6   DEFINING CUSTOMER AND CONSUMER INTERACTIONS

1. David F. Giannetto and Anthony Zecca. *The Performance Power Grid*. Hoboken,
    NJ: Wiley, 2007.

7   IDENTIFYING IDEAL DIGITAL BEHAVIORS

1. https://blog.kissmetrics.com/how-netflix-measures-you/.
2. http://www.hbs.edu/faculty/Publication%20Files/14-020_3553a2f4-8c7b-44e6
    -9711-f75dd56f624e.pdf.
3. http://www.janrain.com.

8   ANALYZING PROFITABLE PATTERNS AND SEGMENTS

1. http://www.nytimes.com/2011/04/11/business/media/11comedy.html?_r=0.

9   ALIGNING DIGITAL INITIATIVES WITH THE ENTERPRISE

1. http://www.agilone.com/case-studies/agilone_cs_petcarerx.pdf.

10   CAPITALIZING ON THE MOBILE MOVEMENT

1. Dr. Emami, Basking Ridge Dental Group, Basking Ridge, New Jersey.

11   DEMYSTIFYING BIG DATA

1. http://en.wikipedia.org/wiki/United_States_Census.
2. http://www.abcteach.com/free/s/science_abacustocomputer.pdf.

12   TECHNOLOGY TRENDS, BUSINESS IMPLICATIONS

1. MediaPost 2012.

INDEX

Join the

Big Social Mobile Movement

@

DAVIDGIANNETTO.COM

Exclusive
Member
Benefits

Case Studies
Industry Examples
Technology Reviews

Additional
information
on action
items within
the book

Worksheets
Workbooks
How-to Guides

SPEAKING ENGAGEMENTS
BLOGS - VIDEOS - ARTICLES